Men
on
FIRE

Also by Stephen Mansfield

The Character and Greatness of Winston Churchill:
Hero in Time of Crisis

Then Darkness Fled: The Liberating Wisdom of Booker T. Washington

Forgotten Founding Father: The Heroic Legacy of George Whitefield

The Faith of George W. Bush

The Faith of the American Soldier

Benedict XVI: His Life and Mission

The Faith of Barack Obama

The Search for God and Guinness

Lincoln's Battle with God

Killing Jesus

Mansfield's Book of Manly Men

The Miracle of the Kurds

Men on FIRE

RESTORING THE FORCES
THAT FORGE NOBLE MANHOOD

STEPHEN MANSFIELD

BakerBooks

a division of Baker Publishing Group
www.BakerBooks.com

Published by Baker Books
a division of Baker Publishing Group
PO Box 6287, Grand Rapids, MI 49516-6287
www.bakerbooks.com

Printed in the United States of America

Library of Congress Cataloging-in-Publication Data
Names: Mansfield, Stephen, 1958– author.
Title: Men on fire : restoring the forces that forge noble manhood / Stephen Mansfield.
Description: Grand Rapids: Baker Books, a division of Baker Publishing Group, 2020. |
    Includes bibliographical references.
Identifiers: LCCN 2019039129 | ISBN 9780801007163 (paperback)
Subjects: LCSH: Men (Christian theology)
Classification: LCC BT703.5 .M338 2020 | DDC 248.8/42—dc23
LC record available at https://lccn.loc.gov/2019039129

Some names and details have been changed to protect the privacy of the individuals involved.

20 21 22 23 24 25 26   7 6 5 4 3 2 1

In keeping with biblical principles of creation stewardship, Baker Publishing Group advocates the responsible use of our natural resources. As a member of the Green Press Initiative, our company uses recycled paper when possible. The text paper of this book is composed in part of post-consumer waste.

To
Jonathan Sandys,
great-grandson of Winston Churchill and dear friend,
who died during the writing of this book.
Everything in these pages,
particularly the references to his heroic ancestor,
are dedicated to him.
Goodbye, Jonathan.

Go forth to meet the shadowy future,
Without fear and with a manly heart.

HENRY WADSWORTH LONGFELLOW,
HYPERION: A ROMANCE (1883)

Contents

Foreword

Scott Hamilton

I remember years ago watching a movie in which comedian Paul Rodriguez had a line he repeated time after time: "It's tough to be a man, baby!" I laughed every time I heard him say it and found ways to repeat it in an attempt to be funny. The crazy thing is—it's tough to be a man!

In my sixty-plus years, I've witnessed how our evolving culture has coerced men to act in certain ways. At times, I feel like I'm back in high school: today we are expected to dress, speak, and live according to whatever our culture tells us is right and acceptable. It's almost reactive being a man today, not intentional. We "stay in our lane," stay out of trouble, and try to stay on course in a world that keeps changing the rules of engagement.

So what does it mean to be a man in our time? The answer to that question is as different for each of us as we are from each other. We all have a distinct identity that gives our lives purpose and allows us to live joyfully and productively. The definition of what it is to be a man will be unique to every one of us. But even saying that, I know that there are parameters to successful manhood.

Culturally, spiritually, physically, emotionally, and psychologically, we need to connect with who we are as men and live it boldly and unapologetically.

For me, growing up the smallest, weakest, and sickest kid in my class, I never felt the power and strength of approaching manhood. I believed I was always going to be bullied and did everything I could to get along with just about everybody. It didn't help that I ended up in the female-dominated sport of figure skating, and you can imagine the challenges I had with my manhood in that world.

So much of our identity as men comes from our earliest days of childhood. In my case, I was adopted by two schoolteachers from northwestern Ohio. My father was a PhD and a professor of biology at Bowling Green State University. He was studious, serious, and an incredibly demanding instructor. He would always say, "No one is taking my class for the grade."

My father's reputation was well known. Once, when I was at a fundraising event for Kristi Yamaguchi's Always Dream Foundation, basketball legend Nate Thurmond was in the audience. I knew he had gone to Bowling Green, so from the stage I asked him if he would answer a question: "Mr. Thurmond, you went to BGSU, didn't you?" He said yes. I asked him if he ever had my dad for biology. There was a long pause, and then he said loudly, "Twice!" It was a very funny moment for the audience, and it reminded me to apologize to anyone who ever took a class with my father. The truth is that my father was strict and difficult to connect with. I loved him, but I definitely feared him too.

My mother was the opposite. She was very much the nurturing type, and I loved her more than anyone in the world. Beloved by everyone in my community, she gave and gave and gave some more. She was the definition of sacrificial. Even while she was going through cancer, she would never give up an opportunity to positively impact everyone around her. She was the one who gave me my view of the world, and I am so grateful for her.

But a man's earliest influences aren't only his parents. In my case, I spent most of my time with my coaches. From the funny and energetic Rita Lowery I learned the value of laughter. Giuliano Grassi was short-tempered, demanding, and ultimately not a long-term coach; sometimes a life lesson is about changing what doesn't work. I idolized coach Herb Plata, but he had health issues—so then I began lessons with 1932 Olympic champion Pierre Brunet, who taught me about integrity and the honest pursuit of perfection. After he retired, I started working with the team of Evy Scotvold and Mary Ludington. Evy was by far the toughest coach I ever had, moderated by Mary's unconditional love. I learned that love tempers everything, even work.

When my parents could no longer support my skating, world-famous coach Carlo Fassi found a sponsor for me, and I moved to Denver to take lessons from him. Later Don Laws guided me to my first Olympic Games, then four US and World titles, and an Olympic gold medal in 1984. Don became family to me but not really a father; he was a private man. This, too, is a valuable life lesson, though perhaps not one I appreciated until later.

From these varied and changing role models, I was forced to sort of make it up as I went along. I didn't know how to approach my life with any real understanding of what it meant to be a man. A real man. The man I was meant to be. There was no all-in example for me to follow. No father figures. Nothing healthy to base my manhood on. Ironically, cancer cured all of that.

Cancer will open your eyes to truth about your life. It wakes you up, strips you down to nothing, and exposes all the junk that's been thriving in time-honored dysfunction. I knew how to do a lot of things at a very high level, but quite honestly, until cancer I didn't know I desperately wanted to be the man God created me to be.

The next chapters in my life have come with a determination to correct my path and become that man. The man I have to be for my wife and four children. And like most men, I remain a work in progress.

Being a man isn't about the illusions mass media presents to us as the way we all should live our lives. Stephen Mansfield is going to make this clear in the pages that follow, and he's going to call you to be the man you are meant to be. You will have to decide, then, if you want your life to be something more authentic, something more beautifully masculine than it is. Here is what I have learned: everything results from a decision. A choice. And this choice is an important one. It can determine the rest of your life.

Dive into the pages that follow. Let the fire come. Then never let it die. Be the man you are made to be.

Scott Hamilton, four-time national and world champion
and Olympic gold medalist

Gentlemen, We Begin . . .

It is not the light that we need, but fire; it is not the
gentle shower, but thunder.
We need the storm, the whirlwind, and the earthquake.

FREDERICK DOUGLASS[1]

My goal in this book is to ignite fires in your soul. I want to recover what has been lost. I want to set on fire again what has been doused. I want to see you live out manhood on fire.

I should tell you what I mean by *fire*. You've likely heard the phrase "fire in the belly." Robert Louis Stevenson gave us these words. He was the author and adventurer who also gave us the classics *Kidnapped*, *Treasure Island*, and *The Strange Case of Dr. Jekyll and Mr. Hyde*. He was using an image probably taken from the practice of stoking a fire in a cast iron stove. The fire was in the "belly" of the stove, and you worked to keep it roaring hot. Today, the phrase describes passion or heartfelt commitment to a cause. A politician, we are told, has a fire in the belly if he carries his campaign to the end. An athlete has the same if he trains hard and gives his all on the field.

I'm grateful for Stevenson's epic phrase, and I want to encourage passionate living wherever I can. Yet when I speak of fire in this book

I mean something more than emotion or passion. I mean something like what the ancients did when they recounted their myth of Prometheus, the titan who stole fire from the gods and gave it to humanity. I'm referring more to the kind of fire that fell upon the first Christians on the day of Pentecost. I mean fire from heaven. Eternal fire that burns in the human soul. Fire that was meant to be a part of us from the beginning and that must be stoked and tended if we are to be what we were created to be.

Let me tell you what you already know. The fire of righteous manhood is threatening to die out in our generation. I will leave debates over the reason for this to other books and to better minds than I possess. Yet I see what you see. I see empty souls. I see men without fire. Men who do not know who they are or what they are meant to be peer back at me on the streets. Sometimes this kind of man also peers back at me from my mirror.

We can blame this on our times if we wish. Manhood is derided as nearly a disease in our day and as the source of many of our societal woes. This taints us. We can also blame our fathers, most of whom failed to pass the lore of righteous manhood on to us or to call out from us the manly heart that is there but sealed away. We have a destiny to fulfill as men, but we were seldom told of it by those who came before us. We have noble purposes to serve, but usually no one sounded the trumpet call, no one demanded that we rise to our manly best.

Still, I do not blame our times or our fathers and certainly not women, who have taken nothing from men that men have not abandoned in the first place. No, I blame us. I blame men. I believe our tribe is at fault for allowing righteous manhood to decline and for allowing masculinity in general to become an object of scorn. I also believe that if we have the power to lose righteous manhood, then we have the power to reclaim it. I believe we will, and in our generation. This is why I am writing these words.

This book is written out of both an anger and a vision. I am angry because of the meager thing manhood has become. I turn on my television and there seem to be two types of men filling the screen. One is IdiotMan, the kind of guy who does a happy dance in a TV commercial because he finally found the remote control in the couch. His wife and children roll their eyes at his stupidity. You get the impression that they can barely endure the fool that he is. This fellow has brothers. They appear in nearly every television program or movie today. They are the way manhood is perceived these days. IdiotMan is too stupid to live, and he ruins his life and everyone else's with his simpleton ways and his self-centered living.

The other man who makes a frequent appearance is DogMan. He's driven by his lusts and his bodily needs. He spends much of his free time watching some scantily clad woman dance around a pole. The highlight of his day is when he can jam a twenty-dollar bill into her underwear. Then he sniffs the air in search of yet another pleasure, yet another sexual moment, yet another place to vent the canine lusts that define his life.

I feel nothing but anger toward these distortions of manhood, because this is what society tells me I am: IdiotMan and DogMan. One is a fool. The other is a wolf.

I am neither. I imagine you are neither too.

What I am is an incomplete man in search of a manly life. What I am is a man determined to find and live masculine greatness before I die. What I am is resolved to slay IdiotMan and DogMan before a watching world and then to gloriously reveal what righteous, noble manhood really is.

ᏵᎧᎧᎧᎧᏸ

It may offend you that I blame men for the demise of true masculinity in our generation. I cannot apologize. Men who do not know who they are and who do not understand the power of noble manhood and the duties of a righteous man are terrorizing our age and destroying themselves. Consider.

- We talk much about the threat of Islamic terrorism today. Yet in the United States it is largely young, white, middle-class, even Christian-associated young men who do the most damage. Men like these are responsible for most high school shootings. It is men like these who have shot up college campuses in recent years. Unfathered, untethered, immoral, angry young men.

- We talk about the plague of erectile dysfunction in our age, and yet much of this is self-induced. Recent studies have shown that much of the increase in erectile dysfunction is due to the use of porn. There is even an acrostic for it: P.I.E.D.—porn-induced erectile dysfunction. Some men are so addicted to the exotic fantasy world of pornography that they can't get aroused on their wedding night when a normal, loving woman awaits. They have brought the sewer into the marriage bed with them. They have rewired their brains through hours of viewing porn and the secret life of masturbation that naturally attaches to a porn habit. Hear me. This wasn't foisted upon men. They did this to themselves.

- Then consider this: the US government tells us that 20 percent of college and university women are sexually abused. Who's doing this? Men. Those same unfathered, untethered, immoral, angry young men. You see, when men don't know who they are, when they are empty and aching and angry, they become predators. They try to force others to fill the hole in their soul. Usually their targets are women. Sometimes they are other men. This has produced a plague of abuse in our generation. It is no wonder that many women do not think of the word *masculinity* without putting the word *toxic* first. Can you blame them?

I could go on for pages, but my goal here is not to merely catalog the crimes of men. I don't believe you can guilt a man to greatness, and this book is all about restoring greatness to modern men. My goal is, however, to get men to stop blaming their times or their fathers or women or whomever for what has befallen them and get on with becoming the righteous men they are called to be.

So, yes, I am angry at what manhood has become in our time. I also have a vision. I want you to have it too. It is a glorious thing to be a man. It is an even more glorious thing to be a man among men. When a man knows his strength and his gifts and uses them to ennoble others, when he understands his needs and satisfies them in righteous ways, he is a thing of beauty. He reflects the glory of God. He assures the magnificence of women. He summons destiny from the hearts of the young. He makes communities safe and nations good and demonstrates virtuous power to the world. Evildoers cower. Weak men recover themselves. Women and children rejoice.

Let's not get too airy here. It's also a blast to be a man! Still, this is true only when that man knows who and what he is and lives masculinity in its full God-ordained power and service.

So we need a restoration of what has been lost. We need to push back on the bilge our dysfunctional age is handing us. We need to stop living from the crotch and start living from a heart where God rules and righteous fires blaze.

∽∽∽∽∽

A few important thoughts before we get started. You will notice a degree of ferocity in these pages. Embrace it. I'm not angry at you; I'm angry for you. I'm like a coach who knows how good his players can be and rages against anything that keeps them from their best. I will hit hard here. I will be blunt. I'm not out of control or incapable of any other tone. I'm not adopting a style to be entertaining. I'm using a tone that good men understand and hunger for. I'm speaking to men about men in manly terms. Don't back away just because my words may not sound polite or conventional to your ears. Polite and conventional aren't getting us anywhere these days. Perhaps we need some friendly raw and hard-hitting words for a change.

A word to women: don't be afraid of this. You have likely been damaged by soulless, demanding, predator males in your life. I'm sorry. Truly. Yet if you will encourage the men in your life toward the vision of noble manhood championed here, it will mean only good for you. You will be loved. You will be served. You will be protected. You will be encouraged and cheered as you fulfill all you are made to be. Toxic masculinity is a disease of our age. Noble masculinity is its cure. That's what we are about here.

Now, about faith. I have spoken around the world with men of nearly every major religion about the need for valiant manhood. I have found Muslims, Jews, Hindus, Yazidis, Sikhs, and men of a dozen other faiths who resonated with me in an eagerness to see a restoration of righteous manhood in our time. They are all concerned about the decline of masculinity in our age. They are all hopeful for the men of the next generation. They are all eager to reach across religious lines to summon men to their best. I say this because each man I talked with knew I was a Christian, was glad I had been open about it, and was eager to learn what my faith had to say to men. So in these pages, it will be the same as it has been in all my conversations with these men. I will be writing as a follower of Jesus. I will be quoting Scripture. I will sometimes be speaking in distinctly Christian terms. Yet I will also be speaking broadly to men in such a way that every faith, ethnicity, race, and background will hear a trumpet call and will, I trust, learn something of the ways of men. Welcome to you, whatever your faith. I'm eager to learn from you too. I'm glad you are here.

One final thought. We sometimes make a mistake when we talk about fire. It is common to list earth, water, and air along with fire as though all are elements in the universe. Fire isn't an element, though. Earth, water, and air are forms of matter. They are made up of atoms. Fire isn't matter. It is a side effect of matter changing forms.

I'll leave further explanation of this to the experts. For our purposes here, let's keep this in mind: fire comes when change happens. It occurs when the right combination of elements takes place and a transformation begins. So it is with your soul. If you, like me, want divine, manly fire burning in your soul, then welcome the change and embrace the transformation that fire brings. Once an ignition has occurred, protect the fire, feed the fire, and tend it as you must so it will engulf your heart.

Let the fire come. Let our hearts be set ablaze. Let manhood in our time be ignited with righteous fire.

So let's get to it.

The Seven Fires

The most powerful weapon on earth is the human soul on fire.
FERDINAND FOCH[1]

We live in an age of data. We should be grateful that we do. Much good comes of it. Yet we have to know the difference between data and knowledge to live meaningful lives.

Data is neutral. Data has no meaning apart from other data. It has no heart, no gender, no faith, and nothing broad and meaningful to deposit in us. It is numbers. It is statistics. It is dots on a screen. We are glad it exists but we cannot let it rule our days.

Knowledge, though, is a bit of creation our minds can digest. Knowledge is alive. It expands in us. It leads somewhere and may have hidden within it a power to change us. Knowledge can make an impartation. It can leave something valuable in our souls.

It is just this kind of impartation that this book is about. You will likely learn some new things here, and this is wonderful. Still, the purpose of this book is to offer only enough knowledge for impartation to occur. We want the mind to learn enough to set the heart on fire. We want to know enough to experience an impartation that causes us to live differently. We are looking for understanding that transforms, that is measured over time by the manly fire burning in the souls of righteous men.

You play a role in this. You cannot be passive. You have to hunger. You have to hope. You have to pull on this meaning and make it your own. Then the fire begins.

Here, then, are the fires this book is designed to ignite in your soul. The tending of the fire afterward belongs to you.

The Fire of Heritage
The Fire of Battle
The Fire of Destiny
The Fire of Friendship
The Fire of Love
The Fire of Legacy
The Fire of God

1

The Fire of Heritage

When a society or a civilization perishes, one condition can always be found. They forgot where they came from.

CARL SANDBURG[1]

Let me tell you about a moment that changed my life.

It occurred in an inner-city gymnasium. I was there because I was accompanying a friend, a young professor of history, who had agreed to speak to the students of a nearly all-black high school. I admired him for doing it. I'm no good at speaking to kids of that age, and I couldn't imagine how he was ever going to hold the attention of an entire gathering of uninterested, somewhat defiant teenagers. I was nervous for him, and he could tell.

My uncertainties only deepened when I saw a kid whom I later learned was named Deshawn walk into the room. He was tall and good-looking, and he entered that gym like he owned it. Laughing with his buddies, nudging underlings aside, he gave several girls a look that said, *Too bad you're missing out on me.*

He then planted himself in the front row. He looked at me. He looked at my professor friend. We were two older white guys in a sea of black youth. We could not have seemed more out of place. Everything about Deshawn's manner said, *You ain't got nothin'*. When a teacher walked up to Deshawn and told him he'd better behave himself, and nothing like what happened last time had better happen again, I knew we might be in trouble. I cut my eyes to the exits. What had happened "last time"? I didn't know, but I was hoping it wouldn't happen between where I sat and the nearest door.

Don't get me wrong here. I wasn't anxious about being in the inner city. I wasn't the least bit uncomfortable about being with black youth. You'd have to know more about my life to know how natural both of these experiences are for me. What was unsettling me was wondering how in the world my somewhat strait-laced professor buddy was going to hold anyone's attention in that barely controlled riot of a school assembly.

The principal took the microphone and quieted everyone down. Then, briefly but graciously, he introduced the visiting professor of history. I couldn't have been more uneasy if I'd been hanging from the edge of a cliff by my toes.

Then it happened. My buddy stood up and said, "I'm here to tell you who you are."

I glanced to Deshawn. I could read his lips as he leaned over to a friend and said, "I know who I am, fool. Who are you?"

I thought for a moment that the uprising might just be beginning. But then my friend—my magnificent, bow-tie-wearing, fearless, learned, kale-eating, whitest-man-on-the-planet friend—just took off.

He said, "I'm here to tell you what people with your skin color have done in history." What followed was one of the most glorious moments I've ever witnessed. The good professor launched into a stirring flyover of black history that made me sorry for all the rest of us.

He told those kids that while his Celtic ancestors were still wearing bearskins in Britannia there was already a sophisticated civilization thriving in Africa. He said that one of the greatest libraries in history was in a city called Alexandria, again, in Africa.

Then he dipped into biblical history. He made sure everyone knew it was an African who helped Jesus Christ carry the cross and that there was a black man among the elders in the church at Antioch, the first great missionary-sending church in Christian history. In rapid-fire fashion, my friend said that the apostle Mark was from Africa, and Origen was from Africa, and Augustine was from Africa too. In fact, he said, all of Christianity was set on its course by the fiery churches of Northern Africa.

"One more thing," he said. "Jesus was from the Middle East, so he looked more like you than he looked like me. Don't you let 'em tell you different."

Now, it was at this moment that Deshawn leaned in. His long arms rested on his boney knees, and his beautiful face fixed its gaze on the professor and wouldn't break away. In fact, a few minutes later he told one of his rowdy friends to shut up so he could hear. I'm telling you, it was a sight.

Professor Awesome didn't miss a beat. He kept machine-gunning facts until he arrived at American history. That's when he told us that the first patriot to die in the American Revolution was a black man. His name was Crispus Attucks, and he was a sailor who gave his life in a skirmish called the Boston Massacre in 1770. We then heard about heroic blacks fighting at Lexington and Concord and Bunker Hill and Yorktown.

My friend kept up this barrage and then ended in a flurry. "I don't even have time to talk about all the black inventors who changed the world. So let me just say this:

"If you've ever used a folding bed, thank a black man named Leonard C. Baily. He invented it.

"If you've ever used a smoker, thank a black man named Maurice W. Lee. He's the creator.

"Have you used an ironing board? Thank a black woman named Sarah Boone.

"If you know anyone who has had their life saved by a gas mask, they should thank Garrett Morgan, the black man who invented them.

"Have you ever received a blood transfusion? Thank Dr. Charles Drew, the black man who created the method for storing blood plasma as well as the idea of the blood bank.

"Know anyone who has had cataracts removed by a laser probe? They can thank Dr. Patricia Bath, the black professor of ophthalmology who invented the device.

"Finally, my favorite: if you love potato chips like I do, thank George Crum. He was the black chef who gave them to us."[2]

Then he closed. "I told you I came here to tell you who you are. Well, these are some of the people you come from. This is what is inside of you. This greatness courses through your veins. Go do things as magnificent as they did."

And then the professor just sat down. This wouldn't have been strange except for the fact that the room had exploded. People were standing and clapping and shouting. A bunch were high-fiving each other. There were teachers in tears. The principal just beamed.

That's when Deshawn did something I have never forgotten. I thought he would just walk out. That's what I had done after every school assembly of my entire life—get out as soon as possible. Deshawn, though, made his way to the professor. He waited his turn. When the professor finally stepped toward him, Deshawn just shook his head up and down as though to say, "That's what I'm talking about," and then he hugged the man. I'm telling you, Deshawn the Coolness put a full-on, head-laying-on-shoulder, not-letting-go-anytime-soon hug on the good Doctor What-Did-You-Just-Do.

When the two let go of each other, Deshawn looked toward me. I nodded, thinking that would be it. No. That wasn't it, because the lanky kid then gave me a crushing hug, and I had done nothing but sit there with my mouth hanging open the whole time the professor had been torching the room.

What I knew was that Deshawn was different after that assembly. He moved differently. He had a more peaceful, happier look on his face. He was ignoring the stir around him and seemed contentedly lost in his new thoughts. Something had come upon him. Perhaps something had been summoned from him. But he was changed, not dramatically but subtly and, I hoped, forever.

The backslapping and handshakes lasted for half an hour before the sound of bells began moving people on. The professor and I then went to lunch with some of the teachers. That's when we learned what that blowtorch lesson in history meant to those students. Only then did I understand the impartation that had taken place. I have never forgotten it.

What had happened? Heritage had happened. A heroic, virtuous, courageous version of the past entered that high school gym and then entered the souls of those kids. They already belonged to families and a race, to a city and a nation, before they joined that assembly. By the time the professor was done, they understood that they also belonged to a people who had endured through time. They were part of something that had begun centuries before them and now continued through them. Their heritage—whatever others had told them—was glorious and valiant and ingenious and powerful. It was something to be proud of and to seek to extend. Almost as important was that a white man had celebrated it and had fiercely insisted that they never forget it.

I'm simply grateful I was there.

The Power of Heritage

Gentlemen, here is the lesson we must cling to all our days. We are made to live our lives with good and noble things from the past flowing through us. We are made to be empowered and lifted by what has come before us, by what has been left to us by our ancestors and by what our fathers and mothers have planted in our souls. In short, we are made to be set on fire by the nobility of our heritage. This is one of the fires of true manhood.

It has been said that a people without a heritage are easily persuaded. It is true, and though this usually is said of nations it is certainly true of individuals. A man who does not know where he comes from, what people and history he belongs to, is lost. He cannot know fully who he is. He cannot know completely what lives inside of him. He is forced to live as though he has come into the world unarmed and alone, as though he has no belonging and has received nothing from what came before him. He must make himself into all that he becomes. He has been given nothing. It is a terrible burden.

Yet when a man knows something of his heritage, it helps him locate himself. He learns that he comes from a people. They had certain gifts. They did noble deeds. They may have done some regrettable things too, but it is the higher things about them that their descendants want to grasp. All that was admirable and powerful and inspiring about this people lives in those who proceed from them. Those living today must make sure the greatness of their people surfaces from within them, illuminates them, and elevates them. The goal is not a narrow tribalism or arrogance. The goal is to allow what came before us to tell us who we are and to lift us to greater heights.

Most men have a visceral need to belong to a tribe, to be a man among men, both past and present. They likely yearn to feel the hands of their fathers upon their shoulders. They hunger for impartation. They long for belonging to a past that lives not only in memory but in the actual heart and muscle of our daily lives.

I once had a dear friend who was a lot of fun to be with. He was constantly joking and playing around. His home life wasn't that happy, and I got the impression that his jovial ways masked some pain, but still I was glad to see him coming.

This friend went into the Marines. When I saw him sometime afterward, he was still pleasant and friendly, but there was a heft to his life that impressed me. He seemed centered and solid in a way he hadn't before. He told me he had found a home in the Marines. I asked him how that differed from the home he had known with a mom and dad and sisters. He said, in memorable terms, that he belonged to a tradition now. He had "been made a part" of what the Marines had been doing for this country since the beginning. I remember that he spoke casually of what "we"—he and his Marines—had done at Tripoli and Chapultepec, at Tarawa and Fallujah.

I realized that the Marines had given my friend a heritage he had never found in his contentious, dysfunctional family. He belonged. He resonated with what had come before. It lived in him. It made him more than he had been.

When my friend wore his dress uniform one day, another friend of ours flipped one of the buttons back and forth with his fingers and made a teasing sound. It was a bad move. My Marine friend knocked the guy's hand away and said, as evenly and fiercely as I have ever heard a man speak, "Don't do that. Ever." It was clear that a fight would break out if it happened again. The offender would lose. For Marines, those aren't buttons. They are the seal of the United States Marine Corps. There is blood and conviction and duty and sacrifice reaching back centuries behind that seal. Don't touch it. Don't dishonor it. Respect what has come before. This and more is what heritage puts in a man.

Claiming a Heritage

We have a problem, though, and we should not try to hide from it. Our problem is that we live in an age when heritage is rarely passed from one generation to another, rarely handed down from father to son. So most men tend to live without the transforming power of heritage in their lives.

This occurs for a number of reasons. One of these is broken families, which leave generational disconnect and resentment in their wake. Another is that we have experienced a succession of generation gaps in which the younger generation distrusts the older generation and doesn't want to carry anything about them forward into the future. The previous generation is seen as too suspect, too flawed, to build upon. A final reason for this loss of heritage is simply ignorance. If parents don't know their past and its meaning, then they have nothing to offer their children. If our schools don't teach the nobility of our history, then we have no story by which to understand the lives of our ancestors. We don't know that the past has mystical power to offer the present.

Now, I want to be very clear about what I'm asking you to do in this chapter. I'm asking you to go claim your heritage. I'm asking you to take what is yours from the past, live out its meaning, and pass it on to those who come after you. I don't want you to stand by, hoping someone comes to you and embeds the meaning of the past in your heart and mind. That's not going to happen. I want you to seize it. I want you to invade the past, *your* past, and take the riches that are there.

Yes, I'm being fierce about this. It is because there is something from your history that belongs to you, and I don't want to see it stolen—not because of family trauma, not because of a culture that ignores the past, and not because of ignorance. I feel the same way I would if I discovered you had inherited a million dollars. I would run to you and plead with you to claim what is yours. Your heritage is worth more than a million dollars. It can transform you. It can transform the people around you. It can empower you to change your world. It can light a fire in your children and grandchildren that nothing else can. Yes, I'm fierce about this, and I want you to be also.

My model for this claiming of heritage is Winston Churchill. I always turn to him when I need the power of heritage reemphasized in my life and when I want to relay this power to others. We know

Churchill as one of the greatest leaders of the twentieth century, but we may not know one of the forces that got him to those heights. It was the power of heritage.

The sad truth is that Churchill's parents neglected him horribly. They were too busy with their aristocratic social life to pay much attention to their chubby, rambunctious son. They left both Winston and his brother, Jack, in the care of nannies and seldom spent more than a few minutes a day with the boys. Churchill's own son once said that "the neglect and lack of interest in him shown by his parents were remarkable, even judged by the standards of late Victorian and Edwardian days."[3]

This was an understatement. The truth is that Winston's father, Lord Randolph Churchill, was descending into madness during much of his boys' early lives. Historians debate the exact nature of this mental illness, but it may have cost the man his political career and it certainly drove him to despise his older son. Lord Randolph thought that Winston was stupid, rarely visited him when the boy was away at school, and thought nothing of telling the adoring child that he would never amount to anything. Winston Churchill was haunted by the specter of his angry, disapproving father all his life.

Rather than collapse under the weight of his father's ire, Winston decided to claim what was his. This began at his father's death in 1895. He might easily have celebrated the man's passing as the end of torment and then lived out a deforming bitterness over his childhood experience the rest of his days. Instead, Churchill decided to dust off his father's tarnished reputation and make the good of the man's life fuel for his own ascent. As he later wrote of this moment, "All my dreams of comradeship with him, of entering Parliament at his side and in his support were ended. There remained for me only to pursue his aims and vindicate his memory."[4]

We must understand that Churchill made a choice. He didn't have to decide to extend his father's legacy. He didn't have to commit himself to honoring his father's memory. The man had been cold and distant and insulting to his son, and no one would have blamed Winston if he had never mentioned Lord Randolph again.

Yet Churchill knew what a father ought to mean to a son, especially a father who was a famous politician, so he simply decided to claim what was his. He made the positive part of his father's legacy his own. He honored it. He spoke of it glowingly in his speeches. He made it a motivating force in his own life.

He did not stop there. Churchill decided to claim the whole of his family's legacy. He spent years researching the life of his famous ancestor, Sir John Churchill, First Duke of Marlborough, who had lived two centuries before, and then wrote a multivolume work on the man. What he learned filled his speeches, many of his other writings, and his life.

No one handed Winston Churchill finely honed lessons from his heritage on a silver platter. No one sat him down and told him stirring tales from his family history meant to inspire him to achieve. Instead, he went after them on his own. He claimed what was his. He took the best from his father's life and then captured the glory from his family's past. He chose to embody it all. He even roared after the meaning of his nation's history on his own. True, he had endured history class as a young man. He'd attended a two-year military school, though, not a university, and had no advanced education in British and European history. He simply invaded the field. He read. He traveled. He drank deeply of what he discovered and made it a part of him.

He was not only inspired in his own soul but was also able to inspire his people with this heritage during the dark days of the Second World War. He spoke to them of their forebears. He spoke to them of their historic greatness, of how it was a gift from generations past. In so doing, he awakened a dormant sense of destiny. In short, he gave them what he had claimed and made his own of the past. Heritage helped fuel Winston Churchill to greatness, and Winston Churchill used heritage to propel his people to their best.

The man even won the Nobel Prize in Literature in 1953 for "his mastery of historical and biographical description." It might just as well have been given for the masterful use of heritage to change the world.

⌾⌾⌾

It is easy to use Winston Churchill as an example. He is one of the most famous men in the modern world. The facts of his life are well known. His rise to fame and power appears almost inevitable when we look back upon him from our time. We might get the impression that all heritage is as easy to discover as Churchill's was—simply a matter of opening books or reading a father's papers.

Let me tell you a different type of story, though. I have a friend we will call Raul. He is happy for me to tell his story, but he has asked that I not use his real name. Raul had tragic early years. His father went to prison for life shortly after Raul was born. The two hardly knew each other. Raul's mother worked herself to death trying to support three children. She died horribly when Raul was only eleven. He was raised by aunts and uncles who had children of their own to tend and who made it clear he would largely have to fend for himself.

Raul was heading toward the way of the streets when a young executives program at the restaurant where he worked chose him for special training. They taught him everything from how to "dress for success" to how to study to how to manage people. Raul excelled. In time, he won a scholarship to college. No one in his family had ever been to college. In fact, Raul wouldn't have even thought of college had his restaurant manager not almost bullied him into applying.

What followed was a tribute to Raul's gifts. Raul went to college, earned a business degree with honors, got recruited by a *Fortune* 500 firm, earned an MBA, married, had children, and lived a good and honorable life.

Yet there was something missing from Raul's soul, and he wisely got some help to figure out what it was. He was a devoted Christian who invested his life in his church and loved his family. He was

33

a respected leader and businessman. He had friends and enough money to buy what he needed. What could be the problem?

He asked a group of men to help him work through this. In time, Raul began to realize that as grateful as he was for all he possessed, he had nothing that had come down from his family line. He had no heritage to build upon. This might not have bothered another man, but Raul couldn't make peace with the idea that he was the first in his family line to really succeed. It felt like a break from all that had come before him. There was no continuity. He brought nothing of his past with him into his success because he had never been given anything of his past. He agonized over the disconnection. What he wanted was anything resembling a heritage.

Raul did not know much about his family history, but what he did know made him proud. He knew that his grandparents, whom he had never met, were migrant farm workers, as their parents and grandparents had been. All the generations before him had spent their lives doing the backbreaking work of harvesting produce. Raul also knew they had loved each other deeply as a family, stayed together through the years, and then died poor. His ancestors had owned little in this world, but Raul saw them as noble and good.

Still, this bit of knowledge gave him little of a heritage, and it did not help that while he was on this search through his past his father died in prison. He was not close to the man, but his father was Raul's sole link to the past. Now that link was gone.

Good came of this sad moment in Raul's life, though. It was while he was claiming his father's few possessions from the prison that he decided to ask a guard a question. "I did not know my father," Raul said quietly. "All my other relatives are dead. Can you tell me anything about him? Anything I might not already know?"

The guard looked at Raul and hesitated. He seemed unsure of whether to tell what he knew. Then the man said, "Look, I know your father was in for murder. And I know he sometimes got in trouble here. It can't be easy being his son. But I want to tell you something hardly anyone knows. Your old man saved up money all year to buy candy for the little kids who had to visit their parents in prison at Christmas. He worked it out with the canteen manager. He did it every year I knew him in here. He'd put a little aside each week, and by Christmas no kid came here on Christmas Eve or Christmas Day who didn't get a little gift your dad paid for."

Raul thanked the guard, shook his hand, went to his car, and cried like he had never cried before. All he had ever heard about his father was how horrible he was, how he had murdered people, and how he had abandoned his family. In Raul's mind, the man was like an evil spirit living in a dark castle called a prison just a few hours out of town. But now, there was one little fact, one truth about his father, that was good and sweet and beautiful. It meant everything.

This one truth about his criminal father became the bit of heritage Raul needed. It was nothing compared to what most people know about their family history, but it was finally something both true and honorable Raul had as his own, something handed down from his father before him.

From this tiny fact, Raul built great good. If the one thing he had as his heritage was a lesson of generosity, he would use it to make something wonderful. He decided to start a foundation to help the poor. Using his extensive business skills, he built an organization that was both effective and trusted. Millions of dollars have poured through this foundation and lives have been changed. It continues to this day.

Here is what I think will touch you most about this. Raul regularly makes speeches about the work of this foundation. Each time, he is sure to say, "My father taught me a lesson about generosity." Then he explains how that lesson from his father led to all the good now being done. Raul does not mention prison. He does not mention the early death of his mother. He does not talk about murder or abandonment or a father he barely knew. No. He talks about his heritage: "My father was a generous man. He taught me lessons of generosity. I'm building upon this gift."

My friend Raul is using the power of heritage to change the world.

My own story of claiming heritage is somewhere between the experiences of Churchill and Raul. I come from a long line of military men. My father was a lieutenant colonel in the US Army who fought in Korea and Vietnam. He was decorated for bravery in war and honored for leadership in peace. My grandfather also served as an officer in the Army. He was temporarily paralyzed during the US assault on Berlin at the end of World War II. Miraculously, he recovered and was shipped to the Asian theater of operation. He eventually served as an advisor to General Douglas MacArthur both in Japan and in the Philippines.

I could go on. My ancestors fought in the First World War, the American Civil War, the American Revolution, and even in the French and Indian War.

It all may sound impressive. Yet most of what I am telling you I learned secondhand after my father died. When he was living, he told me almost nothing. This was in part because he worked in intelligence, and much of what he did was classified. It was also due to the fact that he was of a generation that just didn't talk much about its military exploits. We now know, for example, that some of the men who famously raised the American flag on Iwo Jima during World War II came home, put their uniforms in storage, and never told their families a word about their role in that historic moment. My father and grandfather were part of this tribe. They were either too humble, too pained by the memories, or too unwilling to relive the war in their living rooms to talk about what they had done.

What made this disconnect worse for me was that my military family moved constantly. We relocated a dozen times in my first eighteen years. Though I had loving grandparents on both sides of my family, I rarely saw them. Visits happened only when uprooting from one of my father's assignments and moving to another. A few days once a year was the most I could expect, and though

I adored my grandparents there certainly were no leisurely hours for talking about family lore. I learned little about what had come before me.

When I got old enough to understand the power of heritage, I did what Churchill and Raul did. I claimed what was mine. I was not angry or resentful, but I was determined to take hold of the heritage I knew by then could help me live an exceptional life.

I simply became determined to no longer be the rootless military brat with little heritage, no people, and no belonging, ever putting out vines rather than putting down roots. I refused to live as someone who was spit out of the military system when I was eighteen years old and never had a sense of being in place again. Wherever I might live, I wanted to belong to a past, a people, and, by God's grace, a purpose.

When my father died, I read the official records of his career. I listened to the stories that men who had served with him told me at his funeral. I bought duplicates of his medals and put them in a display case that hangs in my office. A picture of him in uniform sits behind my desk.

I also listened to what my mother and my wife learned in their ancestry searches. I had been told a bit about the war heroes, but now I learned about settlers making the costly journey to the Oregon territory and of farms and ranches that lasted for generations.

None of it was that exceptional in the course of American history, but all of it meant a great deal to me, desperate as I was to belong to something moving through time. These were my people. They had struggled and built, dreamed and accomplished, and all of what they were had a place in me if I was willing. I was. I wanted to live out the goodness and the valor that had come before me.

I should say quickly that in addition to the great deeds of my family there were also great flaws. I could fill a few pages with the divorces, bitterness, racism, and failures in my family history. I don't ignore any of this. I work to rise above it. Still, what I wanted to claim were those forces in my family line that could live in me and make me better than I was alone.

I focused on the good and made it mine. I learned that my father had saved lives in a place called Pleiku during the Vietnam War. I claimed it. I said out loud that I was grateful for my father's heroism and I wanted it to live in me. I learned that my grandfather had been a wise advisor to General Douglas MacArthur, often advocating for the rights of the Japanese and Filipino people. I prayed that this wisdom and compassion might live in me.

And so it went. Anything I learned, anything I admired of what came before me, I worked to make a part of my life. I memorized the stories, told them to my children, recounted them when appropriate to friends, and prayed constantly that what I admired in my family line might course through my veins.

I was also fortunate that my family had preserved treasured objects. In addition to the medals and photo of my father I've already mentioned, a letter opener from my grandfather sits on my desk. My great-grandfather's watch sits under glass in my home. None of these are of much material value, but they speak to me nearly every day of what came before me and of the honor and nobility that I am called to live out.

This recovered heritage has been a powerful force in my life. I often remember the words of the writer of the book of Hebrews, who claimed we are "surrounded by such a great cloud of witnesses" (Heb. 12:1). I ask God to cause their strength to course through me. At challenging times in my life, I have looked in the mirror and said, "I am Stephen, son of Lee, grandson of Kirwan. I am called by God and descended from heroic men. I will not be defeated in what God has called me to do."

Reclaiming Your Heritage

Now, gentlemen, let's talk about you. Perhaps the stories of your family history are well known and much rehearsed. Good. Then take hold of the meaning of what has come before you and make it yours. Learn it. Live it. Celebrate it. Pass it on to others.

It could be that you are more like Raul. Perhaps there isn't much information available to you, and what you do know is more destructive than helpful. I want you to take encouragement from Raul's story. There is something, however small, that you can uncover in your family lore. Find it. Dust it off. Build on it. Tell it to your children often.

It is more likely that your story is somewhat like mine. You have a heritage, you know a bit about it but not much, and you are eager for more. Perhaps you have not claimed the power of what you know or made it yours. Dig in a bit. Ask some questions. Learn what you can. Turn its meaning to prayer and affirmation. It will change you. Heritage always does.

Now, the men I'm concerned about as I write these words are the men who have difficult family lives and who may be too bitter to be willing to face their past and find the buried treasures. Believe me, I understand. Yet I am not asking you to merely say nice things about people who hurt you or who were horrible human beings. I'm asking you to trust that God is always at work in every family line and that there are nearly always diamonds in the dung. I'm asking you to look for God's work and meaning, not to ignore the fact that a drunken father beat you or that, as in the case of one of my friends, you can't name an ancestor who wasn't a crook.

I want you to remember also that a heritage is not always about great battles or being written up in the newspapers. Sometimes it is subtle.

My father rarely said anything to me about me. He could hardly manage to tell me he loved me. He certainly couldn't say the kind of things I say to my children all the time: "I'm proud of you. You really are gifted by God and I'm cheering you on, knowing you'll accomplish great things." These words were not ever going to come from my father's lips, as fine a man as he was otherwise.

Yet during one particularly painful time in my life, a time when there had been great loss and betrayal, my father wrote an email to me and closed with these words: "You will continue to rise." Five words. That's all. If he had never left any other kind of heritage for me, they would have been enough. Those words told me my father believed in me, knew I would transcend that worst moment of my life, and even dared to state this in the form of a blessing.

Perhaps something like this has been said to you. Perhaps all you have is a few words. Then build on them. Perhaps all you have is one small story, like Raul. Take it. Squeeze the meaning out of it. Make it yours. Let those few words launch you. Don't let bitterness keep you from the destiny that awaits.

As you step into this great adventure of claiming the power of your heritage, I want you to consider a particularly exciting truth from Scripture. It is this: often, when God does something new and glorious in the lives of his people, he first urges them to remember their past and remember who they are.

Like me, you may have read the book of 1 Chronicles and found the first nine chapters a slog. This is certainly not the most inspiring part of the Bible. We read who begat who for hundreds of years prior to that moment. Why so much genealogy? The reason is that this is history being written for a people who are just coming out of captivity. Israel has been imprisoned in Babylon for seventy years. They are just returning to their land and reclaiming their nationhood. God is about to do a new thing. First, though, they must remember who they have been in order to carry the purposes of God forward.

It is the same with the genealogies that come before the life of Jesus in the New Testament. We have lengthy lists of "begats" that may be a bit dry to read. In truth, they are the announcement that a great thing is about to occur. The Messiah is coming to earth. All the heritage that comes before him, both in his family line and in the history of Israel, is about to come to its fulfillment. So the mention of righteous people alongside prostitutes and murderers in these long lists is all about to make sense. Jesus comes to give it all meaning. The past truly is prologue. A beginning is being announced in the recollection of history.

The same is true of you. If you have lived a rootless life, disconnected from your history and heritage, it is no accident that you are reading these words. A new season is about to dawn in your life, and it is coming—in part—on the wings of the good things God has seeded into your family history. This is why dusting it off and making that history yours is so essential.

THE BATTLE PLAN

1. Pull together a band of brothers, some friends who know you and who want to help you be the man you are called to be, and tell them what you know of your family background. Ask them to pray for you as you search for the meaning of your heritage.

2. Keep in mind that uncovering heritage is not the same as becoming a professor of history. You are just looking for the stories. You want patterns. You are looking for meaning. Delve into the details only if they interest you. Start by asking questions of the older members of your family. Sit with them and patiently ask them what they know. Write this down and reflect on it.

3. If asking family members about the past highlights a certain period in history, learn about it. If your African American family was part of the great migration north in US history, read a bit about it. If your Native American family members walked the Trail of Tears, learn more. Whatever big events your family participated in, make sure you know about them.

4. Your goal is not to author a book, though you may one day serve your heirs by writing down what you learn. Your goal is to be able to say, in general terms, who your people were. Know the overview. Capture the highlights. Be able to tell the seminal stories. You are weaving a narrative, not writing a dissertation.

5. Keep in mind that internet tools like Ancestry.com and Genealogy.com may prove helpful.

6. Don't ignore the hard truths of your family. Declaring your intention to rise above these troubling facts is just as important as determining to live out the noble features of your heritage.

7. Finally, take the riches of what you learn and turn them to prayer. Ask God to set your heritage on fire in your soul. Invite your band of brothers to be part of this moment. Perhaps ask them to pray that you live out the nobility of your God-given heritage with passion. Determine to keep this fire alive in you all your days.

2

The Fire of Battle

The warrior spirit arises in a man when he loves something or someone more than himself and when what he loves is then threatened.

ANONYMOUS

There is a story that comes to us from the ancient world. It is a story that teaches us about God and warfare and the skills of battle that God wants his people to possess.

It seems that ancient Israel had battled their way into their promised land and won many victories. Under their great general, Joshua, enemies had been conquered and near-miraculous success had been known. The entire land had been largely won.

Largely. Not entirely.

Israel held the heart of the promised land. Nevertheless, along the northern and western boundaries of that land large groups of enemies still existed. They were hostile. Future battles would have to be fought. Israel had been granted an incomplete conquest—not total victory.

Why?

We are told the reason in a preamble to the list of these remaining hostile nations that comes down to us from these ancient times.

> These are the nations the LORD left to test all those Israelites who had not experienced any of the wars in Canaan (he did this only to teach warfare to the descendants of the Israelites who had not had previous battle experience). (Judg. 3:1–2)

There's the reason. The God of Israel did not grant his people a complete conquest because he wanted later generations to know how to fight. He wanted them to have "battle experience." He did not want one generation to win the land and then later generations to be soft and lacking the warrior spirit. These new generations would have to fight, would have to man the boundaries of their heritage and contend with enemies without and within to fulfill God's purposes on earth. So God did not allow the founding generation complete victory. The next generations would have to be warriors too.

Gentlemen, what was true in ancient Israel is true of us today. We are not meant to have our battles won for us. We are not meant to dissolve into softness and luxury because previous generations have won a measure of victory for us. We have battles of our own to win.

This is why one of the fires I want to see blazing in our souls is the fire of battle. It is essential if we are going to be the men we are called to be, and it is the flame that ignites all the others we hope to have burning vibrantly within us.

The Calling of Men to Be Warriors

To be men, to be good and righteous men, we must be warriors. Much of what we are made to do—what we are called to do—is about battle. It is about going to war. To be good men we must fight the battle for self-mastery. We must battle our lesser drives and contend manfully to be the best and noblest we can be. This means war. We are also made to stand at the boundaries of the lives entrusted to us and contend for their good and their destiny. We pray. We fight spiritual battles. At a more human level, we encourage and coach and confront and even discipline. It is all a form of battle. Then we must battle the spirit of our age when it seeks to make us weak and compromising, soft and dull to righteousness.

We contend. We contend in the marketplace. We contend for the prosperity of our families. We contend against unclean things coming down from our family lines. I want the heroism that is in my family line but not the racism. I want the graciousness but not the drunkenness. I welcome the one but war against the other. We contend for good in our communities and contend for the promise of the next generation. This is what righteous men do.

I think you know that the battles I am calling you to are largely invisible ones—over ourselves and spiritual forces and destructive ideas, and for the flourishing of all that is entrusted to us. Still, I don't want to sidestep actual physical battles. We live in an age when fewer and fewer of us will ever serve in uniform. We are not like the World War II generation, in which nearly every American male served in the military.

Yet we cannot let our distance from the martial life keep us from possessing martial skills. I hope you never have to actually fight to keep your family safe, but you should know how. I hope you never find yourself in an "active shooter" situation, threatened by criminal activity, or having to resist a home invasion. Nevertheless, you should know what to do when you are called upon to do it. You should be in good enough physical shape and possess the skills and the tools to stand guard over what is yours. I should too. It is part of what we are made for.

What we require is a restoration of the warrior spirit. Now, I know how this sounds in our generation. In an age in which male violence is nearly a plague on society, me calling for a fire of battle to

45

burn in the souls of men sounds like I'm arming a criminal militia. This couldn't be further from the truth. In fact, the kind of warrior spirit I'm hoping to awaken in men will only make the world safer, children more secure, women better served, and the cause of true manhood more esteemed in our time.

I definitely understand the concerns, though. Sexual abuse is a plague. The trafficking of nearly 48 million people worldwide is largely because some men feel themselves entitled and use their strength to dominate and pervert. Domestic abuse is an abhorrent rising trend, and male violence in general has reached terrifying heights.

No wonder some shudder when I say I want men to be better warriors. Few of the concerned will understand that true warriors contend *for* as well as *against*. Few will understand that the righteous warrior spirit I hope to awaken is principled, disciplined, well mannered, moral, and committed to protect and defend. Give me men of honor who have the fire of battle burning in their souls, and I will give you a more peaceful, more prosperous, happier society.

I know this is true because I grew up in a military culture. My father was a United States Army officer. During my early years, before I went off to college, I lived on a succession of military bases around the world, and I learned some things about true warriors from the experience.

If it is true that awakening the warrior spirit among men leads only to uncontrolled violence and devastation, then military bases ought to be among the most depraved, dangerous places on earth. I never found this to be true. I lived on facilities along with thousands of men and women who were highly trained warriors. Many were armed. All had been trained to kill. Some were specialists in killing, though I doubt they would appreciate those words. Never was I harmed. Nor do I know of anyone who was. This is because a true warrior culture—one that is learned and disciplined and of noble intent—is an honorable, safe place.

I played pickup basketball with Green Berets. If I fouled a man, he didn't snap my neck or pull out a gun. He played on—and usually crushed me on the court. My mother was never molested or made to feel in danger. If she was carrying groceries from the Post Exchange to the car, three men might offer to help. They did this because she was a woman, not because of my father's rank. They wouldn't have known his rank until they got to the car and saw the sticker. My sister walked these facilities in complete safety too. The call to a warrior spirit doesn't unlock demons. It puts them in check. It seals off evil with a protective perimeter of good.

Now, people certainly misbehaved. You can't have thousands of highly charged people living in one place and not have offenses. Soldiers got drunk. They sometimes fought. I'm sure there were crimes I didn't know about. Some I did. I lived in Berlin, Germany, during the Cold War. Once an American sergeant going through a divorce got drunk and drove a tank through Checkpoint Charlie into East Berlin, which in those days was communist territory. That drew some notice, I can tell you!

Yet warrior culture is self-correcting. It knows how to fix what goes wrong in its midst. It knows how to hold its ranks in check. I never knew of a murder, a rape, a theft, or a shooting the entire eighteen years I was a military dependent. Why? Because warrior culture, flawed though it can sometimes be, is rooted in ethics, service, nobility, and punishment of evildoers.

Man as a Warrior

So, what does all this have to do with you? I'm asking you to be a warrior. I'm asking you to declare war on yourself and be comfortable with the idea that much of what a man is called to do can best be described as *combat*. Poets from an earlier age called it "manfully contending." It means that as gentle, as educated, as refined as a man might be, he knows how to take a stand and defend it.

He is confident that he can be fierce when ferocity is needed. He stands guard over those he loves and contends for their good. He spiritually patrols the perimeter of his world and assures that no evil will befall what is entrusted to him. He not only contends *against* but also *for*—for the destinies of his children, for the good of his wife, for the best for his friends, for success in his profession, and for the service of his God. He does all of this because he has first fought the fight for mastery over himself.

We have an enemy in this, and it would be good for us to identify this foe right at the start so we can defeat him. I think this enemy is best described by a single word that is used in the Bible. In 1 Corinthians 6:9, this word is used in a list of behaviors that will keep people from inheriting the kingdom of God. This single word, in the original Greek language of the New Testament, is *malakos*. We get our modern word "malleable" from this word, but it meant something far different when the apostle Paul wrote his letter to the Corinthians.

The word means "to be soft and perverse as a result of luxurious living." Gentlemen, this is our enemy. Softness. Sensuality. Indulgence. Easy living. And all of a kind that leads to perversion.

If there was ever a description of most men in our generation, this is it. If there was ever a description of what we need to fight in ourselves, this is it. Now, you may not think of yourself as mired in "luxurious living." The truth is nearly all of us are. Let me explain.

Though there may be men reading this book who have really hard, nearly subsistence-level lives—and you honor us by joining us in these pages—most of you have far different experiences. You, certainly by the standard of most of the people who have ever lived on earth, are wealthy. You are in the top 1 percent of all who have ever lived. You never lack for a meal. You have a comfortable home to live in. You are not in fear of an invading army wiping you out or a Gestapo-type authority kicking in your door. You carry a magical machine with you—and you hang one on your wall—that allows you, like an ancient king, to summon the most learned advisors and the finest entertainment in the land. You likely earn more than you need just to live, you are seldom if ever in danger for your life, and you can go through each day without ever seriously exerting yourself physically.

You, my friend, are a king by the standards of history.

Don't misunderstand. I'm glad for all you own and all you have at your command. Still, it is exactly because you live such a life that this fellow called *malakos* is your enemy. This condition comes because of our ease. It comes because we live cushy lives. It takes the fight out of us. It allows us to sink into perversion. It deforms our souls and makes marshmallows of our bodies and leaves us far less than what our original purpose demands.

In short, such lives take the warrior out of us. I've been talking to some high school football coaches of late. They have a concern. They love their players but they find their young men to be without fight, without ferocity, without the inner fire and hunger that drive an athlete to his best. These coaches tell me that their guys seem to enjoy being on the field but they certainly are no "beasts," no "fiery champions," no "warriors of the gridiron." They do not know how to contend manfully. They aren't even able to push themselves past pain in the weight room or on the track. In other words, they don't know how to battle.

Why would they? As fine as these young men may be in other areas of their lives, they are nevertheless shaped by ease. They are not desperate for anything: not for success, not for victory, and not for honor. Now, we don't want them destitute and fighting for every meal. We do, though, want them to be warriors in the midst of the abundance they enjoy. It bothers me that their coaches tell me they don't have a single warrior on their teams. And why would they? These boys are produced by a *malakos* culture, one made soft through luxury, one deformed by ease.

These young men are products of our culture of men, and that culture of men in most places on earth is weak and deformed. It is time for that to change.

The Seven Prayers of a Warrior

I want to urge something radical. I want to urge we start with prayer. I believe this is the essential first step in a restoration of the warrior spirit in our lives.

When I make a suggestion like this, I know many men roll their eyes. They are thinking of sweet, lullaby-like, "Now I lay me down to sleep" kinds of prayers. What could prayers like these have to do with restoring the fight to a man's soul? Yet I'm not talking about sweetness and light. I'm talking about warrior prayers. In fact, I'm talking about warrior prayers from Scripture, which means they are prayers inspired by a God who is himself a warrior.

We can't miss this point. Having the warrior spirit restored to our lives isn't going to come from watching war movies and wearing camouflage. It has to start as a work of God. He created us. He intended us to know how to fight the righteous fights of our lives. He alone can ignite this fire in us again.

Now, there are practical things we can do, and we will come to these soon in these pages. Let us first, though, make these seven prayers of a warrior part of our lives. Let's not only learn these prayers but memorize the Scriptures they are based on. Even if you haven't been much of a man of prayer in your life thus far, I think you'll find these prayers drawing you out. These are the words of warriors calling upon their warrior God to act.

The first prayer is this: *Lord, open my eyes to the true spiritual battles of my life.*

We grasp this prayer from a dramatic moment in the life of Elisha the prophet. He is in the ancient city of Dothan with his servant. They are being pursued by an enemy king and his army. When the servant gets up one morning, he sees the city surrounded by the enemy army with all its horses and chariots. The servant freaks out. "Oh no, my lord! What shall we do?" he cries.

Elisha the prophet is calm. "Don't be afraid," he says. "Those who are with us are more than those who are with them."

The servant surely thinks the man has lost his mind.

Then Elisha says the critical words, the words we want to make our prayer: "Open his eyes, LORD, so that he may see" (2 Kings 6:17). Suddenly, the servant can see that there are horses and chariots of fire all around them.

There is our prayer. *Open my eyes, Lord, that I may see*. We need to see the true nature of the battles that are already raging around us. Most men aren't warriors because they don't know they are in a fight. They think only in natural terms, so they don't know an enemy is on the move against them.

A righteous man understands the fight he is in. He understands that darkness is always at the edge of his heart and mind, trying to draw him into porn, into an affair, into addiction, into raging ways and violence, into financial misdealing or a thousand other bondages that would ruin his life. He fights back. He erects barriers. He calls in artillery. He wins.

He even understands the spiritual side of largely natural problems. Sure, a man is overweight because he eats too much and doesn't work out. Still, to gain victory, he has to understand the hole in his soul he's trying to fill with food and also how his invisible enemy has manipulated him in this way all his life. When his eyes are open, when he sees the true nature of his battle, he mans up. He starts to fight. He calls in reinforcements. He uses better weapons. He battles fiercely because he understands that more is at stake than just his waistline.

The good man who seeks to be a warrior asks God to open his eyes to the battles surrounding all he's been given responsibility for. What is the war swirling around his friends or his wife or his children or his business? Our constant prayer has to be *Open my eyes, Lord, that I may see. Show me the battle so I can step into the fray.*

The second prayer is straight from Scripture too. It is this: *Train me and give me skill for the battles of my life*. This is based on the great warrior's cry of Psalm 144:1: "Praise be to the LORD my Rock, who trains my hands for war, my fingers for battle."

We are told in the New Testament that the weapons we are meant to fight with are not the weapons of this world. We are not going to win most of the battles of our lives with tanks and automatic rifles, with air strikes and satellites. While some of us will be forced into natural, physical fights upon occasion, most of our battles as righteous men are of the invisible kind. We will have to fight the pull of depression in the lives of our sons. We will have to battle against body image issues and eating disorders in the lives of our daughters. We will find ourselves called upon to stand with a buddy as he fights his way back from addiction. Our wives may fight bitterness or the torment of abuse. We want to battle at their side. Our communities may be ravaged by racism or sex trafficking or religious conflict or political corruption. We'll want to play our God-ordained role.

I need skills for these battles. I need training. How do I use my words to heal? What role does fasting play? How do I pray? How do I confront? How do I call in help? What practical strategies should be put into play? How should money be marshaled? Which of the thousands of weapons and tactics available to me should I use? And will I be skilled at their use when the time comes?

This is why we pray, *Train me and give me skill for the battles of my life*.

∞∞∞

The third prayer is one of the most important we can pray in this generation: *Give me focus and singleness of heart that cut the trivial from my life*.

We find the basis for this request in the great promise of God in Jeremiah 32:39: "I will give them singleness of heart and action, so that they will always fear me and that all will go well for them and for their children after them."

We all know what happens. As we move through life, we accumulate distractions. Trivial, optional, less-than-optimal obligations attach to us like barnacles to a ship. We live drained as a result. We live with divided attention. We live with too much calling too loudly for too great a part of our lives.

This isn't the way of warriors. The apostle Paul told his young disciple Timothy that "no one serving as a soldier gets entangled in civilian affairs, but rather tries to please his commanding officer" (2 Tim. 2:4). In order to be effective, warriors keep focus. They know their purpose and the complete dedication necessary to fulfill it. Much of their preparation is a process of shedding. They shed pounds, hair, possessions, obligations—anything that weighs them down or entangles them.

I pray often for singleness of heart. I pray it about my relationship with God: *Make me single of heart about you and your purposes, O God.* I pray it about my wife, my children, my calling, the people who I know are in my life for a purpose, and even matters like being in good physical shape and money: *Make me focused and single of heart about your purposes, Lord, and about every battle that is mine to fight.*

❧❧❧

The fourth of our prayers is one of the most honest we can pray: *Give me a willing spirit so I can battle as I should.*

King David prayed this. It was when he was repenting of committing adultery. Among other things, he prayed, "Restore to me the joy of your salvation and grant me a willing spirit, to sustain me" (Ps. 51:12).

You may know the story. One night David was walking on the roof of his palace. He was supposed to be off at war, but he had decided to stay home. He saw a beautiful woman bathing. He fell in love with her. It got worse. He schemed to have her husband killed so he could have the woman for himself.

When he was confronted and became grieved over what he had done, he wrote out his great psalm of repentance. He included the words "grant me a willing spirit, to sustain me." David knew that he had not done the right thing because he didn't *want* to. He wasn't *willing*. He didn't have the desire to do right.

This is a prayer we must pray constantly if we are to be godly warriors serving higher purposes. I can tell you that I do the right things in my life—until I just don't want to anymore. I eat right until I don't care. Then I eat like an elephant. I am kind until I'm unwilling to be kind. Then I'm harsh and caustic. I exercise until I just don't want to. What I need in all these situations and a thousand more is for God to give me the "want to." I need a willing spirit to sustain me.

I know myself. I've failed many times. In each case, a willing spirit would have kept me from simply not caring about doing the right thing. I just didn't have it in me at the time. I wasn't "willing." I wasn't "sustained," and I refuse to be foolish enough to think that the same won't happen again in the future. So I ask for all of my future days and challenges that a willing spirit from God will be given to me to sustain me. I'm praying preemptively. I'm using the long-range artillery of prayer to change situations I haven't lived yet. This is what warriors do.

Give me a willing spirit so I can battle as I should.

◈◈◈

Our fifth prayer is vital. It is this: *Grant me valiant men whose hearts you have touched to battle at my side.*

This prayer is taken from an episode in the life of King Saul. When he was just beginning to rule over Israel, we are told that "Saul also went to his home in Gibeah, accompanied by valiant men whose hearts God had touched" (1 Sam. 10:26).

Gentlemen, this is what you want. You want a band of brothers. You want men who battle at your side and you at theirs. You want comrades at arms who want to be righteous warriors with you and help you take hold of God's purposes for your life.

In short, you want "valiant men whose hearts God has touched." I will tell you frankly that I have lived too much of my life awash in a sea of casual relationships. I have known too many uninvested buddies and too many users and abusers. Now I have a few heroic men whose hearts God has touched to be with me. It has changed everything. They know me as I know them. They are committed to me as I am to them. They are fierce. They will stop at nothing for my good. They are skilled. They understand the knots in a man's soul. They love me but do not fear me. They will risk anything to see me be the man of God I am meant to be, the valiant warrior they know I can be.

This is what you want. I will risk saying this here, and I hope you hear me well: most men have the wrong friends. They have fools and jokers, lightweights and party animals around them. They will never win serious battles if all their friends are men of this kind. Why? Because they will be alone when the day of battle comes. Fools and jokers, lightweights and party animals don't show up to fight for a friend. They always have something else to do.

This is why you must pray this prayer until a band of brothers forms around you that will kick your backside until victory comes. You need men. You need *valiant*—the word means "heroic"—men. You need men whose hearts God has touched. Don't settle for less.

Pray it. Pray it now. Pray it often. *Grant me valiant men whose hearts you have touched to battle at my side.*

⌘

Our sixth prayer is this: *Lord, give me your divine energy as I do your will and fight your fight.*

This prayer comes from the apostle Paul's great declaration that he was determined to "strenuously contend with all the energy Christ so powerfully works in me" (Col. 1:29).

In 2005, I was embedded with US troops in Iraq while working on a book. I spent my days with soldiers coming and going from "across the wire." The guys I was with were going into danger nearly every day. They were real professionals. I saw how they kept their gear and their bodies ready for battle. They knew what they were doing.

One of the things that impressed me most was their almost fanatical insistence on making sure they had enough energy. They were living stressful lives out in the desert for hours at a time. To run out of energy could have meant death. I've never seen such downing of energy drinks and sports goo and vitamins. These folks would "carbo-load"—down vast amounts of carbohydrates—before they went out and then sustain themselves with every kind of energy tablet, pill, or bar while "down range."

It was a lesson for me. I'm a healthy man but I can run out of energy, and when I do I lose my sense of the fight. I make stupid decisions. I'm more susceptible to the immoral and the foolish. Mostly, I'm just weak. No one fights well when he is weak.

To be the valiant warriors we are called to be, we need God's energy coursing through us. We know we will get tired. We know that battles are lost because men grow weary. We want fire beyond our own. We want a divine dynamo, a surge from on high. Red Bull won't do. An energy bar won't get it done. We need an unearthly turbocharge to battle as we should.

I should say too that Paul was probably not just speaking of physical energy. Spiritual things take energy too. Try praying for an hour. Try fasting. Try taking a stand against evil for months at a time. These aren't just physically taxing. They require a kind of divine energy working in our spirits. We need energy at that level too in order to be the best warriors we can be.

We must make this our constant prayer: *Lord, give me your divine energy as I do your will and fight your fight.*

Our seventh and final prayer will probably surprise you. Here it is: *Make my words weapons of godly warfare, O Lord, and free me from what is impure and spiritually damaging.*

We take this from a famous prayer of King David, which asks, "Set a guard over my mouth, LORD; keep watch over the door of my lips" (Ps. 141:3).

It may seem as though we've slipped away from praying like warriors to praying like Sunday school children. Nothing could be further from the truth. In the matter of spiritual warfare, words are weapons. They are what we use to pray, to bless, to rebuke, to encourage, to impart, to inspire, to command, and to instruct. Use them wrongly and we curse, we damage, we discourage, we dishearten, we confuse, and we can even taint with evil. In spiritual matters, words are important things. They are our weapons for good.

We men have a special challenge in using words righteously. We like to joke. We like to talk smack. Some of us like to cuss and tell dirty stories and rip each other up with words that cut like knives and leave ugly scars. This is why we have to pray for a guard over our mouths. It's why we need to station guards at the door of our lips. This isn't Sunday school language. It is godly warrior language.

Think for a moment about the words that have negatively defined your life. They were said by your father or that girlfriend as she was breaking up with you or a coach at an angry moment. You still remember, don't you? Those words have power. They can become a curse. I've recounted many times how a fifth-grade teacher once told my mother in front of me that I was "immature and retarded." It wasn't true, and my friends and I laugh about this now, but I can tell you that I spent decades trying to drive those words out of my soul. They formed a curse that very nearly defined my life. So powerful are words.

Men, take this seriously. It may have been easier for you to pray about seeing battles clearly and having your hands trained for war. I understand. Still, do not neglect this matter of words. It is as though

I have said to you, "Make sure your sword is sharp. Make sure your helmet fits. Test the cinch on your shield so it doesn't fail you in battle." In spiritual warfare terms, talking to you about your words is as important as talking to you about swords, helmets, and shields when it comes to natural warfare. You want to be a skilled warrior? Use your words well.

Pray this with me: *Make my words weapons of godly warfare, O Lord, and free me from what is impure and spiritually damaging.*

So we begin awakening the warrior spirit within us with prayer. Then we turn to the battle over ourselves.

The Battle for Ourselves

If we are going to be good and valiant men, then we are going to have to declare war on our lesser selves. This is how the great men of history thought. They viewed their flesh, their carnal drives, their laziness—a friend calls it the "Stupid Within"—as an enemy to be bested. They used various words for this struggle, but nearly every great man spoke of having to slay the monster within, or having to beat the inner beast into submission, or having to conquer a force within that would ruin him if left unchecked. Understanding this and stepping into the fight is often the beginning of awakening our warrior spirit.

This is hard to do in our age of ease. Our whole society tells us to do what feels good. To seek pleasure. To view anything difficult or uncomfortable as evil. *Go ahead. You deserve it. Slide into that life of comfort.* Yet this is exactly what kills the warrior within. This is what insulates us from being willing to engage in the vital battles of our lives.

Let's get practical. Here is what I am asking you to do. First, build some hardship into your life. Men do best when they are challenged. They rise when they must conquer difficulty. Build this into your life.

I believe, for example, that every man needs to be attacking a performance barrier at all times. This brings a measure of planned hardship and pain. It is good for him. It summons the fight from him and makes both his inner and outer being reach for more. His whole body and soul will start to transform to answer the call.

I can't fully describe the good I have seen this do. I've seen ninety-year-old men challenge themselves to break speed records in walking the mall. I've seen middle-aged men who used to be great athletes start to recover themselves again—wisely! I've seen twenty-five-year-old couch potatoes start to give themselves to an extreme sport. It transformed all of them. An inner warrior arose and began to make itself known in other areas of their lives. While this was happening, the bodies of these men transformed. They found new fire igniting in their souls. They realized that they were not just reclaiming something physically but awakening a bigger force that began to permeate all they did.

I also want you to check out what my friends are doing at ArtofManliness.com. They have programs for men designed to help them awaken the warrior soul. They'll have you conquering new skills, taking cold showers, improving your bench press, lowering your time on a run, and drinking in new ways of thinking. They have challenged me and made me a better man. You'll love the changes they bring to you.

Second, bring this commitment to embracing hardship into your spiritual life. Get up a bit earlier in the morning to read Scripture and pray. Don't see this as something your church asked you to do or as some petty religious obligation. See it as the training of a righteous man. Work fasting into your life. Drop one meal at first, and then over time work your way into an entire day of fasting while you pray the prayers of a warrior we've already talked about. Read books on fasting and prayer. Give yourself to the challenge.

Third, I also want you to start looking at the forces threatening to deform your life as invading enemies. Then I want you to take a stand.

Are you drinking too much? This isn't just something you want and others are trying to deny you. This is an enemy sent to keep you from your destiny. There is nothing wrong with the moderate drinking of alcohol, but if it *has* you—if it doesn't grace your life but threatens to control it—then declare war.

It is the same with the porn that might be pressing into your life. Stop fooling yourself. This isn't a guilty pleasure. It is a stealth bomb sent to destroy you. It is why you might be pulling away from your wife or from normal relationships with women. It is why that other man's wife looks so inviting. It is why your secret life of masturbation is starting to dominate you. Declare war.

There are hundreds of forces that might be pressing themselves into your soul. We've been asking God to open our eyes to the true battles of our lives. Be courageous enough to see what is battling against you. Then declare war.

How do you declare war? The beginning is always the same. Identify the enemy. Go before God to ask for forgiveness and help. Tell some mature friends what you are dealing with. Allow them to confront you and hold you accountable, to pray with you and instruct you. Take practical steps. In fact, take radical steps. Is that late-night porn on TV ruling your life? Then disconnect cable TV if you have to. Is the bar in your friend's home where you are learning to enjoy being drunk? Stop going. Is the vile cussing by a few friends making you a vile cusser yourself? Then step away. Get clean. Get right. Fight the good fight.

I'm going to tell you something that will be hard to hear. For most men, the problem isn't that they don't know how to fight. The problem is that they haven't decided to fight. It isn't hard to get the porn out of your house. It isn't hard to ask for help for an anger problem. It isn't complicated to devise a battle plan for your overeating. You just have to realize these are battles, not entitlements. They are invaders, not pleasures. Get serious. Get help. Get to the fighting. Decide to win.

CRXXC

Now, once you start fighting the battles necessary in your life and necessary for you to master yourself and gain control with God's help, then it will be time for you to awaken to the battles in the lives of others.

There are words sometimes attributed to the ancient Jewish philosopher Philo of Alexandria that will help us here: "Be kind, for everyone you meet is fighting a great battle."

This is how I want you to see those around you. In fact, when a man determines to become a warrior, this is how he begins to think. He realizes that everyone around him is embroiled in a great and decisive conflict nearly all the time. He puts his warrior skills in the service of those whom God has given him. He joins them at the battle lines of their lives. He stands with them until victory comes.

I have a circle of friends. They are dear to me. They are good men, and they are living sterling lives of righteous manhood. Still, each one is fighting a great battle. Is this true only of this particular group of guys? No. It is true of all people. Yet I have committed myself to these men, so I take their battles personally.

One of them—and I share this with permission—is as fine a man as you will want to know. He is a stellar Christian, an exemplary husband, one of the best fathers I've ever seen, and esteemed at his work. What's the problem? My friend battles depression. Like Winston Churchill and Abraham Lincoln and dozens of other great men, he will be doing fine and then a dark cloud will suddenly appear over his life. It will threaten to destroy him. In fact, it will want him to kill himself.

Thankfully, my friend knows what to do. He calls in reinforcements. He gets us comrades praying and hanging out with him and reminding him of who he is. We battle the darkness through fasting and prayer. I'll say this humbly, but I'll say it nevertheless: we always win. Why? Because God is with us, and our friend has men around him who know how to take a stand. We've stood with each other a thousand times. God forbid any of us ever has to walk alone.

Now, what about your friends? What about your son or your daughter? What about your wife?

I love it in the movie *Patton* when General Patton says, "I can smell a battlefield." This is what warriors are like. It is also what I have learned to be like. Because I have battled for my own soul and have good men around me more skilled than I am, I can smell a battlefield. I know what it looks like when my wife or my son or one of my friends is fighting a great fight. I know what it feels like when someone is on the front lines. I run to it. Not with everyone in the world, but with the dozen or so people God has entrusted to me.

Gentlemen, much of the art of manhood—of being a good friend or father or husband or leader—is learning to join people at the battle lines of their lives. Everyone is fighting a great battle. Leadership is joining them. Fathering is in part finding out where the battle lines of your teenage son's life are and manning them at his side. Husbanding is much about encouraging and praying and fasting and standing against the bitterness that wants to consume your wife or the grief that haunts her over the death of a friend.

To do this, you are going to have to take some time. You are going to have to ask some questions. You are going to have to hold a hand or put an arm around a shoulder and ask a tough question or two. You are going to have to stay close.

You'll be able to do all this because you will first have learned how to battle for yourself. You will have learned the skills of fighting spiritual battles for the health of the human soul, but you will also have acquired some humility and some familiarity with the darkness that haunts us all so you can treat the battles of others with love, gentleness, and the requisite ferocity.

⧼⧽

Let me take us home with some extremely practical suggestions for restoring the warrior spirit. Some of these are steps I have taken. Some are tactics men have reported to me and claim made all the difference for them. Make these your own. Customize. Alter. Tweak. Make them work for you. The important thing is that you strategically work warrior passions and disciplines into your life.

First, work some contest into your life. Play a sport. Get involved in some friendly, controlled warfare. Box, do judo, join a soccer league, start games of pickup basketball or football. Do what you can. I have to work out alone because I travel a lot, but I'm always competing with friends using my Apple Watch and iPhone. My daughter—can you believe it!—has won our digital workout competition every time. Even this kind of contest makes me a better man. Do something that means a contest with someone else. Talk some smack. Make a friendly bet. Issue a challenge. Celebrate victories. It keeps the warrior alive.

Second, stay close to warrior culture. Read a few books about war or warriors. Enjoy good—meaning accurate—movies about warriors and war. Let the warriors you know tell you their tales. Stay close to a military academy if you live near one or to the happenings at a local military facility. That said, nothing is as weird as a man who has never served in uniform—and that is certainly me—behaving like he's a grizzled vet. Still, there is nothing wrong with keeping the martial fires stoked in our souls by sticking close to martial culture. It will serve us well in every area of our lives.

I have come into friendship with some Navy SEALs in recent years. I cannot tell you what their example, influence, lore, and coaching have meant for me. I don't want to be them. I do want to absorb their devotion and spirit into the battles of my own life. They have helped me keep the warrior spirit alive and permeating every area of my life. I am better for it. My family is better for it. The men in my life are better for it. I don't ever intend to get far away from the example of men and women at arms.

Finally, let me close this chapter with a vital lesson from the animal kingdom. It is well known among experts that a single tiger will nearly always defeat a single lion in battle.[1] Even though the lion is the "king of the jungle," one-on-one he loses to a tiger every time. Yet it is also true that five lions will always defeat five tigers. You can raise that number from five to a hundred and beyond, and it will still be true. Multiple lions will defeat multiple tigers, though it is the reverse one-on-one.

Why? It is because tigers fight as individuals, but lions fight in teams. Lions work together to take out tigers one at a time no matter how many there are. So, alone, lions are vulnerable. In groups—called *prides*, by the way—lions win because they know how to fight as a team.

Gentlemen, remember this. Only a fool fights alone, particularly in spiritual matters and particularly in matters of his own soul. Remember the lesson of the pride of lions. Fight as a team. Fight as a unit. When you face an enemy, call in reinforcements, call in your band of brothers, and have them join you at the battle lines of your life.

THE BATTLE PLAN

1. Take time aside, perhaps with some trusted friends, to reflect on your life from the standpoint of fighting noble fights. Are you shaped by passive examples of manhood? Does the word *malakos* discussed in this chapter describe you? Why? Did a specific experience knock the warrior spirit out of you? Take stock. Take notes. Be honest. It can be fixed, but you need to achieve "situational reality" before you can make a change. Let the men around you tell you what they see.

2. Even if you have never been much of a man of prayer, pray in the simplest terms the seven prayers of a warrior. You

can just pray the exact words as they are provided in this chapter. At a minimum, pray them as a quick list each day. If you can be part of a group of guys praying these prayers for each other, so much the better. When you can, memorize the verses each prayer is based upon.

3. Make the decision to tell a group of men close to you what the major battle is in your life. Ask them to help. Let them challenge you. You cannot win the battles of your life alone.

4. Think through the people in your life and ponder the nature of the battles they may fight. Talk to them. Ask them where they would say the battle lines are in their lives. Talks like these are optional with distant friends but essential with wives and children. Then, figure out how you can join them in their fight, from prayer to encouragement, from taking a practical stand to holding them lovingly accountable.

5. Decide how you are going to work some hardship and physical challenge into your life. Do it. Get men to do it with you. Get men to hold you accountable.

6. Read up on prayer and spiritual warfare. This isn't something just for women. It is an art of great manhood. Then step into this art as you see the need.

7. Stick close to warrior culture. Enjoy this. Do it with some other men. Always think through how the spirit and devotion, if not the exact skills, of a professional warrior should be part of your life.

3

The Fire of Destiny

Destiny is the push of our instincts to the pull of our purpose.

T. D. JAKES[1]

You likely already know you have a destiny. Most men do. They have sensed it nearly all their lives. It is an awareness that stirs in them. It is as though there is a voice ever whispering, *You are made for something more*. It is a growing certainty of a purpose. A prior design. Gifts have been given. Experiences have been orchestrated. It is all about work that is to be done, an impact that is to be made.

We sense that this is true, but we often feel we live beneath it. This is because we do. Yet this is the greatest confirmation that a destiny exists for us: the grief we feel when we live small and immoral lives and the disappointment we feel when we settle for less. It is also the disgust we experience each time we fail to give our all. Why should we feel such things? Because there is a purpose. There is a way things ought to be, and we know this deep inside of us, in places we sometimes don't acknowledge. Thankfully, we will never be fully content until we see this purpose become a reality.

That there is a destiny set for our lives is great news. It explains much that has troubled us as men: Why am I so uniquely made, so different from the crowd? Because I am made for a purpose, and all my uniqueness, once tempered, will help to bring it about. Why do I see the world differently from others and feel myself so often apart? Because I am made for a purpose, and that cast of mind is part of the perspective that will help me bring change. Why can I never settle, never be fully satisfied in any one phase of life? I believe it's because destiny refuses to leave me alone.

We can rest, but we cannot hide. We can enjoy but we cannot settle. Destiny calls us on—to more, to greater, to deeper, to all that still awaits.

There is certainly a frustration in all of this. Once we accept that we have a destiny, we want to get on with it. As we men tend to do, we want to impatiently accomplish it, and accomplish it *now*. This is just not how it works. As Winston Churchill once said, "It is a mistake to look too far ahead. Only one link in the chain of destiny can be handled at a time."[2] So we have to be content doing whatever is next, whatever our hand finds to do. We have to walk out the progression of destiny step by step when we would rather leap to it all at once. But that simply isn't how destiny is designed.

God and Destiny

This brings us to God. We cannot talk about destiny without talking about God. Indeed, the very idea of our lives being preordained requires the idea of God. Someone had to choose. Someone had to preordain. Choices had to be made. A will had to be exerted. It wasn't the universe. It wasn't brute force or natural law. It was God who chose and crafted and determined long before we were made. Walking out destiny, then, is a matter of synchronizing with God in the fulfilling of his purposes for our lives. This is the grand adventure we are called to as men.

It was this very adventure, this sense that I was made for something God-ordained but unfulfilled, that led me to my faith. When I read Scripture for the first time, I saw confirmation of the destiny I already felt about my life. I had just never known exactly what destiny was, who held the key to it, and how to walk it out.

I soon learned. I began to understand that this destiny is something that was prepared long before I was born. I remember reading the words God said to the prophet Jeremiah, which are true for all of us: "Before I formed you in the womb I knew you, before you were born I set you apart" (Jer. 1:5). I had always felt like a misfit. The possibility that I was an accident made more sense to me than the idea I was intentionally created. Yet constantly throughout Scripture we are told that each of us was known before birth, that we were designed for purposes determined before time.

King David took the whole matter further. He wrote entire songs celebrating God's choosing and prior design, and how all this began to be fulfilled before he was born. David thanked God for making his "inmost being." He spoke of being "knit . . . together" and "woven together" in the womb. He claimed that at God's hand he was "fearfully and wonderfully made" (Ps. 139:13–15). When I first read these words I was a gangly teen with oversized feet and a body that had never been a fit—anywhere! To think of it all having a purpose was liberating. I realized then that the only misfit things about me were things I had done to myself.

David also threw in a clincher: "All the days ordained for me were written in your book before one of them came to be" (v. 16). I can almost recall the exact moment when this truth first settled into my soul. My days were ordained. My life had an architect. There was a definition already determined. The insecurities and fears that had shaped my life began to give way. I started to see then what I better understand now: a destined man ought to be a confident man. A destined man is not alone. There is a God bringing his life along according to a plan. I haven't been the same since.

Sometime later I stumbled upon these words: "We are God's handiwork, created in Christ Jesus to do good works, which God prepared in advance for us to do" (Eph. 2:10). The word *handiwork* in the original language means "work of art." So we are works of art, created by God to do grand things he determined "in advance," meaning before time began. Something began to stir in me when I read these words. It was a sense that while I should do my best and strive to fulfill my purpose, good works had been prepared for me. Put another way, successes had already been predetermined. Virtuous deeds had already been planned and put in my path. I would need to give myself to them when they came, but their accomplishment did not all depend on me. God had decided they should occur. He had a plan. I felt peace in this. And rest. My destiny was not in my hands.

It was also true, though, that I had to want my destiny to be fulfilled. I had to strive for the good that was preordained. The apostle Paul captured this attitude when he wrote, "I press on to take hold of that for which Christ Jesus took hold of me" (Phil. 3:12). Paul had certainly been taken "hold of" in a decisive way. When Jesus famously appeared to him on the Damascus Road, Paul heard these words: "I have appeared to you for this purpose" (Acts 26:16 NKJV). God had taken hold of Paul so that he could in turn take hold of a purpose. It was the same with me, I understood, and so I began yearning to see destiny unfold in my life.

I had no great theological conflicts about free will as opposed to predestination. I wasn't smart enough for such things. What I was beginning to know was that I made some choices and that some choices were made for me. It was a mystery I would never fully understand. I didn't care. I just wanted to fulfill my purpose, to take hold of my destiny. Also, to know God was near.

I liked, though, that Paul assured a group of people who were concerned about him with these words: "[Don't] be unsettled by these trials [that we are enduring]. For you know quite well that we are destined for them" (1 Thess. 3:3). Ah, so even hard things can have purpose in our lives. I loved this. It meant that hard things weren't necessarily screwups; they weren't always just tragic accidents that left only devastation. They could be ordained. They could be used. They could be part of the plan.

For years the pieces of these truths floated in my mind like so many birds in chaotic flight. Woven in the womb. Knit together. Purposes determined before birth. Known by God before conception. Created for good works. Suffering is sometimes ordained. Press on to grasp a purpose. Chosen. Called. Destined.

When these truths first came to me, I felt as though I was wearing someone else's clothes. Nothing seemed to fit just right. Everything seemed far too large for the still-unformed man that I was. In time, though, it all began to solidify into a certainty. It started to fit. It started to permeate. It started to form itself into a condition of heart and mind.

It did not produce haughtiness but rather a calm humility. Deep gratitude filled me as I began to walk in this world as a man chosen, body and soul, for good works in this life. There was peace. There was confidence. There was a fiery determination to see eternal purposes fulfilled in my life as much as it depended on me.

Destiny and Great Men

It was as I drank in these truths and let them do their work in me that I began to understand what a sense of destiny had meant to men in history. Everywhere I looked in the past, on nearly every page of the books I read, I saw men acknowledging their debt to a divine purpose that ruled in their lives.

I saw it in the life of Churchill first. He once told his wife that over him "beat unseen wings."[3] He also assured her, "There has to be a purpose to it all. I believe that I was chosen for a purpose far beyond our simple reasoning."[4] When he became prime minister of the United Kingdom at the start of World War II, he later said, "I felt as if I were walking with destiny, and that all my past life had been but a preparation for this hour and for this trial."[5] Because he knew the power of destiny in his life, he could speak to his nation in terms like these: "The destiny of mankind is not decided by material computation. When great causes are on the move in the world . . . we learn that we are spirits, not animals, and that something is going on in space and time, and beyond space and time, which, whether we like it or not, spells duty."[6] A strong sense of destiny undergirded Churchill's greatness, and we should be grateful that it did.

I saw the same in Douglas MacArthur, who repeatedly exposed himself to enemy fire during World War I, certain that God would protect him so he could fulfill his purpose. Later, during World War II, when General Eisenhower took command away from a misbehaving George Patton, what tortured Patton the most was that he might not be able to play his destined role in the great conflict of his day. Thankfully, he eventually did.

Martin Luther understood his life as destined too. He once wrote of the great Reformation then unfolding, "God alone is in this business. We are seized so that I see that we are acted upon, rather than act."[7] Luther felt propelled forward by the purposes of God. Great things were unfolding, but they were not Luther's doing alone. He was merely playing the role assigned to him. He was merely walking out destiny.

Even in times of great agony, men have understood that destiny ruled. When the great Booker T. Washington was leading his people after the terror-filled years of slavery, he proclaimed, "I believe he [the ex-slave] is destined to preach a lesson of supreme trust in God and loyalty to his country, even when his country has not been at all times loyal to him."[8] The white man may have done his worst, but God had greater purposes. Destiny ruled, even after the abuse of an entire people.

So it has unfolded, page after page, great event after great event. Men have been powered in their lives by an unswerving sense that

God fashioned them for a purpose and that his purpose would prevail. In most cases, this is what made them bold. They sailed unknown seas and fought mighty foes and carried truth into dangerous darkness and stood their ground in great moral contests, and did so fiercely, all because they were sure they were destined. It is not going too far to say that a strong sense of destiny has powered much of human history and certainly much of human valor.

Destiny and You

This, then, has been my experience, and the experience of some famous men. What about you? Please hear me about this. There is no truth of destiny that is not true of you. There is nothing in the pages of Scripture about a God who chooses purposes for us in advance that is not true of you. As hard as it might be to believe, there is nothing about destiny that is true of Churchill, MacArthur, Patton, Luther, Booker T. Washington, or any other great man or woman that is not true of you.

The question is whether you are willing to believe it and then fight for it, whether you are willing to allow your life to be defined by a fire of destiny burning in your soul. It is not an easy thing to believe. We are told the opposite by the voices of this world, by our failures, and even by our own laziness and irresponsibility.

I return to where I began with this chapter. You surely already sense in your inmost being that there is some purpose for your life. You may believe you have derailed it by the way you have lived, that your past deeds have disqualified you. That isn't true. You likely sense that there is a purpose. You may even be able to look back over your days and see the patterns of providence in your life: the serendipitous moments and the deliverances and the turning points that no man could have engineered. These are signposts for you. They are evidence that God has been at work. What is important is that you are willing to accept God's claim on your life and you are willing to pay the price to live out the grand adventure of your destiny.

If you are, then let's get on with looking at what you must do now to begin allowing your life to be defined by what has been ordained for you.

Protecting the Sacrifice

First, the man who knows he is destined keeps his life clean and free so that he can be prepared for his purpose. This is about more than just morals and manners, as important as those are. It is about staving off the forces both within and without that try to put us in bondage and ruin our lives.

There is a beautiful image of this that comes to us from the ancient world. It is a tale of one of the greatest men who ever lived. His life is the foundation for three religions. His deeds are recorded in some of the oldest documents of human history. His name was Abraham.

Now, according to this story, Abraham was disturbed because he did not see things unfolding as his destiny required. He was frustrated and concerned. The exact issues don't need to concern us here. What we need to know is that Abraham complained to God that things were not as they needed to be for destiny to be fulfilled.

God responded, according to this tale, by telling Abraham to meet with him and to make a sacrifice. Abraham did. He went to the appointed place, sacrificed animals as was the custom, and waited for God to act. It was at this moment that birds of prey—we should picture them as huge vultures—began to descend on the sacrificed carcasses to devour them. Quickly, Abraham drove them away (see Gen. 15:1–11).

It is a simple image, but it is one we should take as a warning if we are going to live as destined men. Abraham is holding a sacrifice before God that concerns his destined purpose. Still, before God answers, before the fulfillment comes, enemies try to destroy the sacrifice. Abraham has to protect what he has offered to God.

Gentlemen, in the matter of destiny, we are the sacrifice. Our lives are what we offer to God so a purpose can be fulfilled. We have to protect these lives and drive off every destructive force so that we can stay untainted and ready for service.

This is one of the most important truths we can know about living destined lives. When we commit ourselves to God's purposes, when we determine to live out a way chosen for us, we put a target on our backs. The simple truth is that evil seeks us out and tries to destroy us. Call it what you will. The devil. Other small-minded human beings. The demons in our souls. Our own corrupt human nature. Whatever you name it, evil comes, and it comes to dominate us so we cannot or do not serve our greater design.

I am often asked what the common factor is in the lives of the great men I have known and studied. I'm quick to answer. It is that they have had to fight through horrible evil done to them or that they did to themselves in order to rise. They were abused as children. They were abandoned by their fathers. Depression haunted them. They gave themselves to drink or sex or drugs or crime or violence or a life of lies. Their pain made them abusers or it made them hate. They were tormented.

Why? Why is this nearly always the case? It is because the destined are targeted. It is because with great purpose often comes great pain. We have to know how to drive off the birds of prey.

We have to know this truth or risk missing our purpose. I remember sitting with a few extremely talented and famous music artists in Nashville. I told them I was honored to be with them because they were likely the best in the world at their art. They inspired me, I said. Immediately, they told me this wasn't true.

They then began telling me about people they had known who were far more talented than any of them. It turns out that the greatest guitarist was not the famous rock star with all the albums and concerts. It may be a guy this artist knew who could play like an angel but could never stay sober. And the greatest pianist who may have ever lived died young of an overdose. The greatest drummer? According to these men, he was in prison for the rest of his life for having killed his wife and child in a drunken rage.

These were apparently the best. None were better. Their talent was stunning. Yet they never fulfilled the purpose for which they were given their gifts. Evil took over. The birds of prey came to devour. No one drove them away.

So a man who understands himself to be destined looks at any force attempting to dominate him and sees it as a possible barrier to his purpose. He doesn't see porn as an entitlement or a rage problem as just a family trait or addictions as just pleasures that maybe go a bit far. He sees them as enemies sent to conquer, and he drives them off. He gets the help he needs. He declares war if he must. He does all he can to keep the sacrifice of his life clean for his purpose.

If history is any guide, it will not be lack of talent that will keep you from being what you are called to be. It will not likely be lack of education or money or will. No, you are more likely to be kept from your purpose by destructive forces you welcome into your life than anything else. You have to stand guard. You have to have good men and women around you. You have to live by a code of conduct that keeps you clean and available for your purpose.

Serve the Season

A second guiding principle for our lives is to serve the season we are in. We must live to the full all the requirements and demands of each phase of our lives, each stage. This is how advancement comes. It is the way we are prepared for our purpose. It is the way we prove ourselves to God and humanity and show that we are ready for more.

I wish I could tell you that destiny descends instantaneously in dramatic experiences and then we are all set. New life begins. Everything happens at once. Ultimate destiny is immediately ours.

It ain't so.

The truth is that the purposes for our lives emerge slowly, precisely. They ooze forward, taking shape over time and through natural processes. The art of the fulfilled destiny is for a man to understand that his life is the school of his destiny. He is being prepared through everything he lives through every day. This is why he has to give himself to every season he finds himself in.

Read the lives of great men. You can see the layering of experience in their lives. It's easier to see in their lives than in our own. They move from season to season, from condition to condition, each layer embedding something in them that they will need when they step onto the ultimate stage of their destiny. We admire it in their lives but often resent it in ours.

Consider Abraham Lincoln. He worked his family farm as a boy. While he did, he read voraciously. When he came of age, he left home and ran a store. He handled the mail. He became a small-town lawyer. He never attended law school. He read the law and was approved by other lawyers. His reading on the farm prepared him for his career in law. The one built on the other. He then started traveling to try cases. He got to know the common people of his state, their needs and way of thinking. Then he ran for the state legislature. He won. He listened. He learned. He made good use of the folksy manner he had adopted in small-town trials. In time he ran for Congress. He was in this role less than a year. But he learned. He opened a law office. Not long after, he started building a national reputation as a speaker. His reading, his trial work, his years in the state legislature, and his short time in Congress prepared him for it. And largely on the strength of his fame as a speaker, he became the president we know and love. You can see it, can't you? Each phase of life schooled him for the next. Each layer of experience prepared him for the one to come.

I could describe the same progression in nearly every life of consequence. It is the same for you. In fact, this entire truth is captured in some words spoken by Jesus. Try to hear them as advice on how to achieve and not just a child's Sunday school lesson.

> Whoever can be trusted with very little can also be trusted with much, and whoever is dishonest with very little will also be dishonest with much. So if you have not been trustworthy in handling worldly wealth, who will trust you with true riches? And if you have not been trustworthy with someone else's property, who will give you property of your own? (Luke 16:10–12)

You see the guiding principle in this. Be honest with little, and you'll be entrusted with more. Be trusted with natural things, and true riches will come. Take good care of the property of others, and you will earn property of your own.

The layers of experience you go through in your life are your opportunity to prove yourself in all these things and to acquire skill. It's why presidents once flipped burgers and prime ministers once waited tables and generals once peeled potatoes and billionaire CEOs once slept in garages while learning their trade.

There are two things, then, you must be sure to do. First, do not become frustrated. Do not let yourself grow exasperated with the fact that destiny does not arrive soon and all at once. The unfolding of destiny is a process in God's hands. It will feel like it moves at a glacial pace. Have confidence and do one of the hardest things for gifted, destined men to do: be patient. Remember Churchill's wisdom: "Only one link in the chain of destiny can be handled at a time."[9]

Our second task is to give ourselves fully to each season in our lives. Don't hold back. Live to the boundaries of your responsibilities. Do what you do well and with passion. Learn what you need to learn, tend your duties well, go beyond what is required. Mine every season for what it's worth. A new season will soon dawn. You'll need everything you've gained from the season before. Remember: slackers lose. The devoted receive even more to be devoted to.

Live the Examined Life

The third principle for seeing destiny fulfilled will sound odd, but it is vital. Keep an eye on yourself. Live an examined life. Watch what emerges in your soul, your interests, and your opportunities as you go through life.

The truth is that destiny comes at you like a curve ball. It is rarely what you thought it would be at the beginning. The wise man keeps an eye on the changes. He watches the contours of his life. He keeps track of what emerges in him as he moves forward. Destiny moves us from what we've known and been sure of to the new and sometimes unfamiliar. We should be glad it doesn't all depend on us, but we also have to keep watch to serve it when it comes.

This is the reason most people don't end up working in the field they studied in school. I have a friend who trained as a dentist but who pastors a church today. I have another friend with a degree in literature who now runs a highly profitable tech firm. How many times have you heard someone at the top of their game say, "I never set out to do this. I was very happy doing something else."? Destiny flows through our lives and gives them a shape we might never have expected.

We have to keep watch, then. We have to see the newly open doors. We have to be aware when the chosen career is no longer a fit or we've lost our heart to a good cause or we find gifts emerging we never had before. All of this is possible when we declare ourselves for fulfilling a purpose chosen for us. This is the adventure of destiny.

A final thought on this: the wise man knows he doesn't see himself clearly. Even the image of himself he sees in his mirror isn't fully accurate. He needs the eyes of others on his life. He needs the perspective others bring. Many a productive new direction in a man's life has come because someone noticed his new skills or new heart for a cause or opportunities he didn't see. Don't walk alone in this matter of destiny. Trust your band of brothers. Trust the wise women in your life. They will see things you don't see. They will know you in ways you don't know yourself.

Remember, a lion fighting alone always loses. A lion fighting with a team always wins. Be the lion in his pride. Battle for destiny with a team of men devoted to your good, as you are theirs. This is how the possible comes.

Grow Your Gifts

There is a fourth truth that positions us for our destiny, and it is one we see clearly illustrated in the lives of great men through history. It is this: grow your gifts. This may sound trite, and it may sound like motivational-speak, but it is what destined men do.

There is much flawed thinking about human gifts in the world today. Most people believe they fall from the womb with certain aptitudes, and these aptitudes then define their lives all their days. They gravitate toward math or technology or medicine or teaching because this was the kind of brain they were given on the assembly line of heaven before they were born.

Now, I will leave what happens in heaven before we were born to better theologians than me. Experience and observation tell us, though, that whatever intellectual leans we might have in life, we acquire other gifts and skills as we live. The wise man, the destined man, pays attention to these as they emerge and grows them as best he can. He knows these might be gifts from God. They might be part of what he is ultimately made to do. However his gifts might unfold, they are part of him, and he wants to live as a man fully alive and fully developed in order to be all he can be in this life. This is the way of men who know they are destined.

The marks of this kind of thinking in history are amazing. I always turn to Winston Churchill first. We think of him as a writer, a speaker, and a leader. None of these came first or naturally. He was born with a lisp and had to conquer it. He was also slow in school. He read and learned on his own. He started out as a terrible speaker. His first speech in Parliament was a humiliating defeat. He stayed with it. He knew he had some gift for oratory and he grew it. Friends often saw him pacing in the woods, giving speeches to the birds and the trees. He also taught himself to write, largely by reading mountains of books.

This wasn't all of it. Later in life, he learned to paint. He said it helped him to see reality better and made him a more effective leader. His paintings hang in art galleries to this day. He also taught himself bricklaying and even earned the appropriate license. The grounds of Chartwell, his family home, are still adorned with evidence of his bricklaying skills. Winston Churchill grew his gifts.

So did Theodore Roosevelt. He taught himself taxidermy and boxing and cattle wrangling and even military science. We think of him as the grand Colonel Roosevelt leading troops up San Juan Hill in Cuba during the Spanish-American War. That is true. Yet he had never served in uniform before then and learned all he knew about military science from books. It turned out he had a gift for military affairs. When he realized this, he developed it. This became part of his role in the world. Theodore Roosevelt grew his gifts.

I could list similar examples by the hundreds. There were astronauts who discovered great gifts for teaching late in life. A prime minister discovered a gift for cooking and used it to build bridges in the divided politics of her country. Some great leaders of the past suddenly discovered an aptitude for learning languages they had never recognized before. They gave themselves to it and made it part of their leadership lives. One famous global leader picked up the piano in midlife. He later used his playing to win adversaries over and move hearts to join him in his cause. Another man took up carving. He was good at it. He would carve beautiful figures while he met with officials and then give them his work as a gift. It won people over and helped him serve his country.

Let me use a slightly less exalted, more contemporary example. One of the men I admire a great deal today is Shaquille O'Neal, the famous seven-foot-one American basketball star. I certainly esteem him for his amazing sports career, yet the main reason I respect him is for what he has done since his basketball days. He could have simply retired and rested on his laurels. Instead, he's grown his gifts.

He has earned a legitimate doctorate at a major university. He also graduated from the Los Angeles police academy and became an officer. He did this to help heal his community. He has acted and sung and done voiceovers for major movies. He's a leading broadcaster. He's also one of the most astute and successful entrepreneurs in the United States today. He invests wisely, buys assets, grows businesses, conducts a school for entrepreneurs, and has become one of the most in-demand speakers in American business today. He also, like his friend and fellow player Magic Johnson, transforms troubled neighborhoods with his investments. We can be fairly sure Shaq did not possess all these skills when he was a star on the court. Instead, he recognized new abilities emerging in his life. He got help to mature them. He grew them over time. The growth of some gifts fed the growth of still other gifts. Now he is having greater success, visibility, impact, and fun than ever. Why? He grew his gifts.

You will experience much the same in your life. You will feel new interests emerging. You'll notice new skills pressing against the surface. You may even find yourself hungering to develop abilities in the very areas of your life where you experienced embarrassing failures earlier on. Give yourself to it. Grow your gifts. Pay attention to what you feel emerging in your soul and draw it out. In short, give God as much to work with in your life as you can.

God and Men

Now, for our fifth and final truth, let us return to the place we began. We started by talking about God.

Some of you have come to this book filled with faith and are delighted when I talk about God in these pages. Some of you are hesitant, perhaps burned out and offended. Others hope it is all true but have lived a life of religious disappointments. You just aren't sure anymore. Some are mystified that I am even discussing religion in connection to manhood in the first place.

I understand it all. I do.

I have to state the truth, though. Your destiny lies in the hands of God, and here, at the heart of this truth, is one of the greatest opportunities for you as a man. Let me explain.

If you have given much thought to religion at all, you have probably perceived it as something that requires you to conform. Most religion seems to most people like a program of behavior management, and so it is natural that religion seems to shout loudly to a man, "Why don't you just behave yourself?"

I want to offer another perspective. If it is true, as I strongly believe and have said in these pages, that God made us and he made us to be men, then it may also be true that he wants to relate to us as men. Notice I'm not talking about religion or church or doctrines or duties. I'm talking to you as a man and saying that there may be a big adventure for you to live out in connection with God that will be the most thrilling aspect of your life.

What if living in a relationship with God isn't castration? What if it isn't like the surgical removal of every drive and instinct we've ever had as men? What if, instead, God wants to enter a relationship with us in which he meets us exactly where we are as men? What if in this relationship everything starts to fall into place, and we find ourselves living with all pistons firing and all purposes for being men fulfilled?

Let me keep going. What if this is what the women in our lives have been waiting for? What if our sons have been desperate for us to stand up and show them the way? What if the hearts of our daughters have longed for fathers who are true men and who give them all the love and protection and guidance and fun they can handle? What if the world is waiting for men who walk unashamedly with God and say so, and yet who haven't been neutered or tamed or overly domesticated?

I say it is true, and it is time for you to resolve this matter. Here's the bottom line: God made you. He likes you. He wants you to be fully male. He wants a relationship with you. He wants to do genuine manhood with you.

So it's time for you to take long walks and talk to him. It's time for you to chat with him on the way to work. It's time for you to ask him to help you be a man. It's also time for you to realize that in this aspect of your life, as with all others, you need other men. Real men. Men of faith. Men of God. Let them speak to you and challenge you and call you up higher. Go find them. And don't settle for anything less than being part of a body of faithful people who are building righteous, loving, powerful men.

◦◦◦◦◦

Now, what does all this have to do with destiny? I say again, your destiny lies in the hands of God. You've heard me urge you to protect the sacrifice of your life and stay free from the evils that seek out a destined man. You know I want you to serve every season of life you find yourself in, to live an examined life, and to grow your gifts. Yet if you do all of this apart from connection with God, the God who fashioned your destiny to start with, then you are merely engaging in a self-improvement project.

You want more, though. You want the designer to build out his design. You want the purpose-setter to fulfill his purpose in you.

The ancient Celts called God "the Destiny Weaver." They were ferocious warrior/poets and they knew God as both Warrior God and Artistic God, as both the fierce ruler of heaven and earth and the weaver of beautiful designs. He wants to be both in your life and to answer the cry of your warrior/poet soul. This is how destinies are fulfilled.

A final word about this. You will have to fight for this thing called destiny. It does not come easily, particularly not in this age. You'll have to fight to maintain your connection to God. You'll have to fight, as I've said, for mastery over your behavior. You'll have to fight for all that your destiny ought to mean to the others in your life.

Let me hit this harder. You'll also have to fight the discouragement and the doubt and the frustration every destined man and woman feels. To believe in a destiny is to believe in a life that means something special and is set apart. This sets us up for hope. This puts expectation in us. This makes us dream big. It also means that we can sink into disillusionment when life doesn't measure up to the promise. Fight this. Fight it off. Call in your faithful friends. Charge them to remind you who you are. Devote yourself to reminding them as well. Defeat the depression of the valleys before you reach the heights. Everyone who has ever taken hold of their destiny before you had to do the same.

THE BATTLE PLAN

1. Take time aside to quietly ponder this matter of destiny in your life. What makes you feel that there is a purpose to your life? Are there moments or turning points in your past that have shown you this is true? Write these down. Perhaps process this with faithful friends.

2. Also process with faithful friends where you are with God. Can you see him as the ancient Celts did, as the Destiny Weaver? If not, why not? Have there been wounds or disappointments or

doubts? Bring these out. Be honest about them. When you are done, if you can, ask God to draw near. Tell him you want all that it means for his purpose for your life to unfold.

3. What does it mean to you to protect the sacrifice of your life? What "birds of prey" have come for you in your past? Against what, exactly, will you have to stand guard? Discuss this with faithful friends. Ask them to walk with you in this.

4. What does "serving the season you are in" mean for you? What does it mean for the season you are in now? How can you serve your current season fully? Again, ask faithful friends to help you and hold you accountable in this.

5. Think through how you will live an "examined life," how you will keep watch over yourself for the new directions that emerge. Ask faithful friends for their perspective and help.

6. In the same way, take stock of your gifts. Have you had to "grow" them? Are you willing to grow them further? How would you do this?

7. A challenge for you: you must walk out your sense of destiny without making it a source of haughtiness and the center of your life. You must also walk out your destiny in recognizing and supporting the destinies of your family and friends. Think through practical strategies for this. Get the perspective of faithful friends. Don't let an arrogant approach to your destiny become your downfall.

4

The Fire of Friendship

Friendship is not something you learn in schools. But if you haven't learned the meaning of friendship, you haven't really learned anything.

MUHAMMAD ALI[1]

Let me tell you one of the most moving stories I know about men and friendship. It is a tale of two soldiers, two armies, a great war, and a bond between men that would not die.

The first of our men is Winfield Hancock. He was born in Pennsylvania in 1824. He later received an appointment to attend West Point, and upon graduation was made an officer in the 6th US Infantry. Hancock served in Minnesota and Missouri, eventually landing in California. He married, had two children, and rose in the Army on the strength of his courage and a seemingly supernatural gift for military life.

He was the kind of man who ignited the souls of those who followed him. In his later years, his troops called him "Hancock the Superb." Ulysses S. Grant would remember him in his memoirs as "a man of very conspicuous personal appearance. . . . His genial disposition made him friends, and his personal courage and his presence with his command in the thickest of the fight won for him the confidence of troops serving under him."[2]

Our other man is Lewis Armistead. Born in North Carolina in 1817, Armistead was rougher and more fiery than Hancock. He too received an appointment to West Point, but he lacked both the grades and the bearing to remain at the school. He was so combative that he once broke a plate over the head of a fellow cadet named Jubal Early, a man who would eventually become one of the nation's foremost generals. West Point dismissed Armistead. Still, his father helped him get a commission in the Army. He landed, then, as a second lieutenant in the 6th US Infantry. This is where Hancock and Armistead met.

Though both men would rise in the ranks and become generals, Armistead's life was filled with tragedy of a kind Hancock never had to suffer. Armistead married Cecelia Lee Love, a distant cousin of Robert E. Lee, and had two children with her. One of these children died in infancy. Cecelia died the same year. Two years later Armistead's home burned down. A year after this he married again, but his second wife died miserably in a cholera epidemic.

Hancock and Armistead were friends for seventeen years. They bore the weight of military service together. They helped each other endure. When Armistead was tortured by grief, it was Hancock who spoke the words that brought relief. It was Hancock who took the unneeded glass of whiskey from his distraught friend's hand. Armistead stood at Hancock's side as well, advising him, encouraging him, and being the friend that a man needs when on assignment far from home.

They would part with the onset of the Civil War. Hancock returned to Pennsylvania to fight for the Union. Armistead, a son of the South from North Carolina, pledged his skills to the Confederacy. There was no bitterness between them. Some accounts of their goodbyes have Armistead telling Hancock, "Win, so help me, if I ever lift a hand against you may God strike me dead." In another, Armistead simply said, "Goodbye. You can never know what this has cost me."[3]

They would never meet again. Yet they wished to, and almost did. Time and again they asked after each other. Several times they petitioned their superior officers to visit each other under a flag of truce. It was common practice at the time. Permission was granted, but these battlefield meetings never worked out. So the two men were sustained in war by memories of the manly affection they shared.

They nearly met on the third day of the Battle of Gettysburg in July 1863. During the famous Pickett's Charge of that day, the Confederate Army marched a mile over open fields to puncture the Union line. General Armistead was part of that Confederate force. He knew that his friend General Hancock was waiting with his men on the other side of that field. He knew Hancock would never yield. Still, Armistead charged on. His brigade was the only one that made it all the way to the Union lines. It was then that Armistead was shot in the leg while climbing a barricade. Moments later he was hit again, and then again. He sat down against the wall. Not too far away, General Hancock was shot on his horse as he encouraged his men to continue the fight.

Armistead knew he was dying. He asked a Union soldier if General Hancock was near and could come to him. The soldier happened to be one of Hancock's aides. The man apologized. General Hancock had been wounded. "Tell General Hancock," Armistead said, "that General Armistead sends his regrets."

General Lewis Armistead died on July 5, 1863. Hancock, though, recovered from his wounds. He rose in society and later ran for president. He died in 1886. Never did he forget his friend. Never did he cease speaking of the depth of friendship the two men had known.

Throughout the years after the war, Hancock's most treasured possession was something he received not long after that day at

Gettysburg. His wife had given it to him. It seems that shortly after the two generals parted company that last time in California, Armistead gave instructions that, should anything happen to him, his Bible was to be sent to Hancock's wife. Not long after Gettysburg, the Bible arrived at the Hancock home.

There is today a monument at Gettysburg. It is on the south side of the great battlefield at the National Cemetery Annex, just where Taneytown Road crosses Steinwehr Avenue. It is called "Friend to Friend." The stirring statue that adorns it depicts General Hancock's aide cradling the dying General Armistead as he asks for his friend. The story of the two generals' relationship is told on a plaque. A second plaque speaks of how Hancock and Armistead's "bonds of friendship enabled them to remain a brotherhood undivided."

My God, these were men! Think of it! These men knew such a bond of friendship that distance, war, and a divided nation could not end it. In fact, they had such a friendship that a monument was built to celebrate it and commend it to generations yet unborn. I say it again: these were men!

The Decline of Male Friendships

I think of these two men often. I think of what they shared and what it has meant through time, and I often turn my thoughts to prayer for the men of my generation. The truth is that we need what their story offers us. Men are in crisis when it comes to friendship in our time. We need to understand it so we can make a change.

You have likely read the same headlines I have, headlines that report the surveys that tell the tale. Most men in the Western world today cannot name a best friend. The average man not only cannot name a best friend but also cannot name anyone he would call if he was out of town and his son was put in jail. Who could he trust with such a thing? The average man doesn't know. He also doesn't know who he would call to help his wife at three in the morning if the dog has run away or a child is in crisis or the pipes have broken and the house is flooding. Who would you trust to go to your house in the middle of the night when your wife is in her pajamas and she's panicked and needs comforting? Most men have no such friends. Do you?

It gets worse. The male suicide rate is skyrocketing in the Western world, particularly in the United States and Britain.[4] When the psychological postmortem on these deaths is done, we find that the cause is nearly always loneliness. The suicide notes tell us that these men ended their lives because they felt no one cared, because they had no man who was close enough to make a difference in their lives.

I am saddened by these facts but not surprised by them, given the progression that most men live out today. Let me describe it. When they are young, say in elementary school or high school, friends come naturally. You remember that time. We are forced together seven hours a day in the classroom, and then there are the sports teams and the music groups and the parties and the proms. Friendships seem automatic, almost effortless. We meet, we bond, we hang out, we think it will last forever.

It does last—for a while. Perhaps we join the military or go to college. Again, candidates for friendship are readily available. It all takes no work. The sinews are already there, the common interests are there. Life is good, as it is in our early working years when the drink after work and maybe the pickup hoops are all we need to bond.

Then life takes over. We marry. We have children. We acquire a house and a mortgage and several cars. It is all wonderful. It means, though, that we get busy. Then we get isolated. We get turned inward, into our private worlds, and we lose what was once so readily there with other men.

It is in his late thirties or early forties that our average dude wakes up and realizes he has no friends. What he has left are "rust friends," the term psychologists use for the buddies we once had but who have been nearly lost through neglect. A rust friend is that guy who was in your wedding but whom you haven't talked to in five years. He was your roommate in college or the Army but you haven't heard from him since. You love him. Or at least you love the memory of him. You still laugh when you think of your escapades together. Yet rust friends don't know if you're in trouble. They don't celebrate your successes. They can't challenge you to your best. They simply aren't near.

This is the state of most men today. It is no wonder we are in such decline. It is no wonder that more of us are killing ourselves every day. It is agonizing to walk alone in this world. To live with no close friends is to live a bleak and tormented life.

A Hunger for Friendship

Gentlemen, we are made for more. We are made to have men in our lives who inspire us with their spirit and their coaching and their belief in us and their fun and their drive. We are made to be close to men who make us better merely by the thought of them, merely because we remember the covenants we've made and the challenges we've issued and the expectations they've lovingly laid on our lives. We are meant to laugh and hurt and yearn and strive and—yes!—achieve because we have a noble band of brothers.

Let me tell you one of the most pitiful things about our tribe of men in this generation. It is the way that we almost worship manly relationships on movie screens but don't have them in our lives. This is pitiful! And, trust me, I was the most pitiful of all.

I remember how I felt when Doc Holliday says in the movie *Tombstone* that Wyatt Earp is his friend and that is why he's fighting at his side. Another cowboy says, "Hell, I got lots of friends." There's a pause. Then Holliday says, "I don't." I remember to this day how I wept. Why? I knew I wasn't even as well off as Holliday. At that time, I couldn't name one friend at whose side I was willing to fight and die, or he for me.

I've watched men fix each other in *Seabiscuit* and rescue each other in *Saving Private Ryan* and coach each other in *The King's Speech* and make each other better warriors in *The Last Samurai* and battle for each other in *Braveheart* and stand for each other in *Black Panther* and help each other overcome bitterness in *The Count of Monte Cristo*. My heart nearly bursts each time. I wanted it. I wanted all of it in my life. I didn't want to just visit manly friendships at the movies once in a while. Still, I didn't have any of it in my life at the time.

Perhaps I should be grateful. Perhaps when we see the power of manly friendships and the glory of what men committed to each other can achieve—even if it is only in a movie—it stirs a hunger in us. Perhaps it increases our sense of need for more than we have and makes us less willing to be satisfied with our tragic isolation and loneliness. If it helps to build a fire in us, I'm all for it.

There is a sad fact that has also helped to build a bigger fire for manly friendships in me. I'm an Army brat who has never served in the military myself, so it was a huge honor to receive the Pentagon's permission to join the troops for a while in 2005 when I was working on a book about soldiers and faith.

I spent long hours with men and women on the front lines. I talked to the wounded. I sat in debriefings with those fresh from the field. I listened to special forces units just back from action, and I talked to senior officers who were trying to stay on top of a complicated battle plan.

All of this moved me to love veterans even more than I did already and to try to understand their challenges as well as I could. This is what brought me to one of the saddest truths I know.

I spent some of the best hours of my life with young vets back home, but I always noticed a reticence in them. I could tell there was something they felt but couldn't say, and I assumed, at first, that I was the problem. I hadn't served in uniform and so they couldn't fully talk to me. No problem. I hoped someone else could draw them out.

In time, though, this changed. Some of them began opening up. With tears they told me that the secret they didn't feel they could talk about openly was that they wanted to go back to war. They wished they were back in uniform, back with their unit, and were about to roar down Route Irish in their Humvees once again. They were guilt-ridden by this wish. What kind of animal wants to get back to war when he has a beautiful wife, loving children, and the life he has always dreamed of? This is how they thought.

When I pressed, I discovered the reason these vets wanted to get back to the fight: they had never known friendships with other men as they did during their time at war. Not before they went and not since they returned had they ever known such bonds with other men. However lovely their family or rewarding their job now that they were home, they were lonely. They wanted what they had once known. They would have given up all that they enjoyed if they could be back there with a role and a purpose and a band of men to fight for.

Gentlemen, think about what this means. Friendship and the rich company of men is so hard to experience in this world that some men would be willing to risk being at war again if they could know once more the depth of friendships they had on the battlefield.

This is beautiful, sweet, and tragic. It just shouldn't be this hard.

Knowing this increases the fire in my soul for manly friendships. So does what other men have meant in my life.

I had a good father, but while I was growing up he was busy with his military career and often away at war. My only brother is nine years younger than I am, so there was frequently no one around to teach me about being a man. Since we moved nearly every year, I learned at each new assignment to lean into the tutoring of other guys my age. They were already familiar with the new post, already knew where the movie theater was and which dads would take you on their motorcycles and how likely it was that any of us would make the school football team. I made my way because other guys taught me.

When I left home and went off to college, it was much the same. I remember that I showed up at my university not knowing how to shave. I had only used an electric razor. All that stuff with shaving cream and razor blades and something called aftershave was foreign to me. It seemed like magic. One evening, an older friend taught me how to shave. I was eighteen and felt stupid, but I had already learned much of what I knew from older guys and saw no reason to stop.

During these same years, I learned manners and how to play racquetball and how to impress a date and how to dress 1970s cool and how to lift weights and how to balance a checkbook—all from other men. I even learned how to study through the patient tutoring of an older student who had served in the Army and was willing to help a young knucklehead get through a tough school.

The point is that other men had me. They watched out for me. They taught me what I needed to know. They didn't let me mess up too badly. I felt safe. I felt mentored. I felt like they had my back as well as my best interest at heart. Sure, there were times when their coaching drew blood or embarrassed me in front of that particular girl. But I learned. I got better. I thrived during my university years, but not because I showed up ready to excel. It was because I had learned from my years as a military brat to rely on the counsel of other men. I also learned how to be the kind of man other men could rely on.

All of this makes it even more incomprehensible that I ever let men drift from my life. I did, though. I followed the typical male pattern of letting marriage and children and houses and jobs keep me from my band of brothers.

Let me be clear. It wasn't the fault of my wife or my children or my financial obligations or my job. I recommend all of these to every man I know. No, the problem was that I started thinking I was too busy for close friends. I might get a bite to eat with a guy, but invest in a band of brothers? Give myself to other men fully so that we all became better together? If you had asked me, I would have told you I believed in it. Deep inside, though, I naively thought I had outgrown it all.

So, when a crisis came in my life, I was largely alone. I had no band of brothers. I had no lifetime friends. Nearly every man I knew at the time either worked for me or was part of the organization I ran. Most of them drifted away.

I had built stupidly. I had fallen into the great male trap. There were no men who would go to war with me when the battle came.

Fortunately, a new band of brothers formed around me. They protected me. They challenged me. They exposed the darkness in my soul. They taught me manly lore I had never known. I walk with them still, and I cannot fully express what they mean to me. Still, I regret every day that I ever let the lessons of my early years and the example of all great men slip from my life.

We are better together. We need each other to thrive. We must do life with a band of brothers, or we will fail to be what we are meant to be. These are the lessons I learned at great cost, and these are the truths we must restore to the culture of men in our time. The fire of manly friendship must burn brilliantly in our souls.

Now for the good news. We can build manly friendships. We can have the band of brothers that we need. This isn't a matter of chance or being born with the right personality or having a talent that draws people or being blessed with wealth. There are skills you can master to begin having heroic men in your life. These are part of the manly lore we should have received from our fathers. Most of us didn't. Still, we can reclaim what we need, build wisely in our time, and pass these skills on to the generations that follow us.

Here is the target. Let me state very specifically what you want to build to see virtuous manhood achieved in your life and the lives of the men around you. I could call it simply a band of brothers, but some may not know what this means. I want to be specific. I'm going to tell you what your goal is and how to build it. Ready? What you want is a Free Fire Zone. The way you start is with Indirect Connection. The way you transition from one to the other is by Calling in Reinforcements.

The Free Fire Zone

The very heart of what you want with a core of men around you is what I call a Free Fire Zone. No, I didn't invent this phrase. You may know that this is language used in the military. It has to do with the conditions that govern how freely men in battle can fire at an enemy.

I'm not using these words in quite the same way. I use the phrase Free Fire Zone to describe a condition among a band of men in which anything that needs to be said to make any one of them better will be said. It is a state in which a group of men have agreed that they are committed to each other's good and that they will address anything that needs to be addressed in a man's life to help him be his best.

Not only will these men speak to the issues in a man's life but they will then join him in his fight. They will coach him if they can. They will get him coaching if they can't. They will pray for him, hold him accountable, and cheer him on until victory is achieved.

This Free Fire Zone is agreed to by men who love each other, enjoy being with each other, and have fun and rowdy times together but also keep an eye on each other to help each man be all he is meant to be. This privilege of addressing any matter is never abused. It is never used to hurt a man or to allow anyone to feel superior. It is used sparingly, gently, wisely, compassionately, and encouragingly.

Though I describe men being in for the long haul with a man's problems, most of the matters confronted by a band of brothers are quickly dealt with when someone simply has the courage to step up. It doesn't take much at all to deal with a man's rudeness to his wife or foul language or lateness or laziness. It might take longer to help him with his grammar or his wound from his childhood or his weak fathering. Yet even these start getting better when someone just has the boldness to speak.

I don't mind telling you what men have dealt with in my life so you can see how this works. In my adult years, I have had my band of men talk to me about my impatience, about my anger toward another man, about my harshness during an appearance on CNN, about being too much of an introvert, about my workouts and weight, about pride, and about how much I was on the road and away from home.

My guys also check on me from time to time, just as I do them. I happen to like Oreos. A lot! It has become a code word among my guys. When I'm traveling, one of them is certain to work into a phone conversation, "How are you doing with the Oreos?" He isn't really concerned that I am somewhere eating thousands of Oreos. The word *Oreo* has come to mean all of the excessive eating I'm tempted to do on the road. People are kind to me as I travel and graciously feed me too well. If I'm not careful, I can gain serious weight. My guys know this because I've told them so. They've also got eyes. They can see my stomach getting bigger and my clothes tighter. And so they check on me. "How are the Oreos? You eating too much? You gettin' your workouts in? You on top of it?"

Don't think it stops there. Though I've never had an episode with a woman when I'm traveling, my guys check on me in this area as I do them. They'll ask if anything has come up on the road. They'll ask if porn is any kind of problem, though I have no particular problem with porn. They're going to ask anyway. I'm grateful. I want them to. Anything is open to them.

All of this comes out of time we've spent digesting good books for men, talking about how to be a righteous man in our age, and agreeing on principles good men ought to live out. Our band isn't a Bible study or a book club or an intervention group or counseling session. It is whatever we need to help each other, all with a lot of fun and nonsense along the way.

So, the Free Fire Zone is the goal. What is the method?

The Indirect Connection

The skill that every man must learn is the art of the Indirect Connection. This is the key to manly relationships, and it is the way that even the most self-conscious, introverted guy can begin building a life with other men.

The Indirect Connection is a way men can connect with each other without having to be directly emotional or disclosing, at least not initially. It is an event built around the way men best size each other up and step into relationship: while something else is going on.

This is all based on the way men naturally relate to each other. Men don't get to know each other best by describing themselves to each other. This is what most men's groups are based on, and it doesn't work that well. The worst thing you can do to engage most men is to circle up a bunch of chairs and say, "Bob, why don't you tell us how you're feeling right now?" You might just as well drop a stink bomb in the middle of the room! No self-respecting man enjoys this kind of thing.

Instead, men get familiar with each other and, hopefully, comfortable with each other while they're doing things other than talking. We take note of how that guy watches a football game and handles it when his team gets clobbered. We size a guy up by his manner with other men, his willingness to jump into the work, and his capacity for fun and the joking that always happens whenever men gather. We watch. We notice. We take mental notes.

We are also aware of things we are hesitant to mention. If a guy heads home before cleanup is done, we notice. If a guy talks about himself all the time and seems eager to impress, we notice. If he is all hat and no cattle, as they say in Texas, we also notice. It is the information we use to determine how close we are willing to let any of these guys get.

This is what men do, and we do it from an early age. Researchers do studies with little girls and boys. They put them in a room with toys and other children, first two girls and then two boys. The girls will eye each other for a while and then inevitably move two chairs facing each other. Then the girls start relating to each other, face to face, eye to eye, talking all the time.

The boys, though, almost always move the chairs side by side, shoulder to shoulder. Then they start looking for something to do together. Notice: they get to know a stranger by doing something together. One challenges the other to a race. The other suggests they shoot water guns at Tommy. They then decide to see who can build the coolest fort with blocks. You know how it goes. You've done it! Again, this is simply the way of men.

It doesn't change when we get older. It is just that the Indirect Connections aren't provided for us as they are in our younger days. We have to create them ourselves.

This is wonderful news, though. It means that bonding with other men isn't the privilege of the highly social few. It is an art every man can master. Any man can grill up some burgers before the game and have a dozen guys over. Any man can schedule a drum circle or call some guys together for cards or order up some pizza after a pickup basketball game. There are as many variations on this theme as your creativity allows.

I've known men to schedule monthly fishing trips and others to create an indirect connection around poker. One guy I know simply bet five other guys that he could cook up better ribs than any of them. This contest went on for six months. My guy lost. He knew he would, but he built a band of brothers out of the experience in a town he had moved to only a few months before.

So men start to connect and then they start seeing who's up for going further. You will have friends who never want to go beyond the touch football game and the beer. No problem. They still make your life rich and you theirs. But a few will show interest when you tell them what you're reading or ask them about the most important lesson anyone ever taught them about being a man.

You build on this. While you're casting that line into the lake or waiting for the second half or catching your breath after hiking that hill, you keep giving them a chance to step into the subject of righteous manhood with you.

It would be just about the same if you were trying to find out if they hunt or if they play an instrument or if they have any interest in going to the concert next month. You bring it up. They respond. You bring other stuff up next time. This is what it means to draw people out. This is the art of the indirect connection. The important thing is that the indirect connection allows you to hang out with other men and have a blast all while getting a sense of who might want the aid of some good men in becoming a better man himself.

So your target is the Free Fire Zone. Your initial method is the Indirect Connect. What then?

Calling in Reinforcements

What moves you from building friendships through the Indirect Connection to the glorious intensity of the Free Fire Zone is what I term Calling in Reinforcements. This is when you ask a man you already know to help you with something he's better at doing than you are. It is the moment you enlist a man's aid in being a better man yourself in some arena where he excels.

You want to be careful here. We are not trying to manipulate. We are also not trying to bring the man into the core of our lives too suddenly. Instead, you want to move the friendship, naturally and casually, toward being helpful as well as fun.

Some years ago, after I had gotten to know a man in fun and manly ways, I began noticing what a fine husband he was. When I heard him talking on the phone, he would always use a pet name for his wife. He wasn't the least bit embarrassed to be speaking in such terms in front of me. He once asked her if he could do anything for her that day. We were standing on the racquetball court at the time. I knew of no other man who would offer such a thing to his wife while other men were waiting. He seemed genuinely in love, but it was his manner with her that drew my notice.

When I met his wife, I could see her total delight in her husband. She really loved him and was thrilled to see him coming. They weren't weird about it, but they had a serious romance going on even in the midst of all the busyness that children and successful professional lives and a special-needs mother-in-law could visit upon them.

The man obviously had skills I didn't have. So I asked him to help me. Would he teach me what he knew about being an exceptional husband? I told him I'd make it easy on him. He could insist I read a book via a single text. He could instruct me briefly. I was a quick study. I wasn't wanting to add to his burdens. If we got together to eat, I'd be happy to buy. "Just open up a little time in your life to teach me," I said.

He did, and he did it mainly by inviting me into his home. Over dinners and at family Ping-Pong contests, I observed and then literally took notes once I got home. Later, we would discuss why he did a certain thing or how he came to understand what he did about his wife. This only went on for a matter of months, but it changed me. I still have much to learn, but I was moved dramatically forward in the journey toward being a good husband by getting this man to mentor me for a short while. I'm grateful every day for his imprint on my life.

What had I done? I called in reinforcements. I got help with an area in which I was in need and he had strength.

Here's what happened then. At just about the same time we were winding down my tutoring, he got a promotion that required he do a good deal of public speaking. The whole idea made him sweat! He had never been a good speaker and knew he needed help. He also knew that speaker training is something I do. He said he didn't want to impose on me, but could I help him become a better speaker? Given all he had imparted to me, I was happy to. I became the mentor and he the mentee. It was easy. The connections and trust were already there.

Now, I mention all this because our friendship went from the sports, workout, and food stage to a "let's help each other get better" stage over a period of months. We had both called in reinforcements for some challenge we faced. It was almost natural that we would eventually talk about what we were each doing to be better men. When we did, we realized that we both wanted the same thing: a group of fun guys pushing each other to manly excellence. This man is one of my band of brothers to this day. I couldn't be more grateful.

Calling in Reinforcements moves a fun friendship to a new level of help and support. It isn't meant to abuse another man's generosity. It isn't meant to cannibalize a relationship. It is meant to move a friendship toward something deeper than fun and rowdiness without losing the fun and rowdiness. It is meant to take two friends and make them allies. In time, they can be something even more.

◌◌◌◌

Let's restate the Big Three. What we want is a Free Fire Zone. The way we start is the Indirect Connection. The way we transition from one to the other is by Calling in Reinforcements.

Gentlemen, were the situation in our generation not so desperate I would not risk being so practical. I would simply say, "Go out and make friends. Eventually, make some of them your band of brothers. Have fun!"

Still, all the evidence of our times is that men have not been taught the basic skills of friendship, and so most walk alone. Moreover, without friendships there are no allies, and without allies there cannot be the band of brothers that every man needs. We can change this trend in our time.

Here is the bottom line: I want you to have friendships like General Winfield Hancock and General Lewis Armistead had. I want your life filled with the joy of manly company. I want you comforted and protected and guided and inspired by the men you draw close around you. I want history to be changed by what you do together. I even want monuments to be built to your friendship—if not on a battlefield, then in the hearts of your children and in the lives of those entrusted to you. I also, by the way, want you to have a heck of a lot of fun through the years.

We can change the dreadful statistics of our age. We can turn the deadly trends. We can be men transformed by manly friendships.

THE BATTLE PLAN

1. Find some time to take stock of your history of friendships with men. Have you had great friendships in your life? If not, why not? Do you still? If not, why not? Think this through with a few guys you pull around you. Let them do the same.

2. Have you ended up following the usual male pattern of friendships? Do you have "rust friends"? Are they all you have? Honestly describe to yourself and perhaps a few others where you find yourself now in friendships with other men.

3. Does the idea of a Free Fire Zone scare you? Why? Have you ever had it with a group of men? Are you willing to start taking steps to have this dynamic in your life now? What are those steps?

4. Are you already doing the Indirect Connection with other men? If so, in what way? If not, how can you start? Have some men hold you accountable for making these types of connections.

5. What would you have to offer other men if they were to Call in Reinforcements from your skill set? In which areas of your life would you Call in Reinforcements if you could?

6. Set a timetable. You cannot schedule relationships, but you can schedule the Indirect Connection. You can schedule your intent to scout out other men to build friendships with. Write it down. Commit to it. If you are a man of prayer, commit this plan and hope to God.

5

The Fire of Love

You see, it's not just that a man needs a battle to fight. He needs someone to fight for.

JOHN ELDREDGE[1]

You have probably made a manly fire or two in your life. So have I. It is something men love to do.

It may have been in the woods or a backyard firepit or in a fireplace in your home. It doesn't matter. The ritual is much the same. You prepared the space, smoothing out the ash from previous fires, perhaps building a circle of stones to protect it. Then you laid in a gathering of kindling or paper or leaves. You followed this with a cathedral-like structure of logs.

It was time to light. You put a match to the kindling. Perhaps it went out. You tried again. If you are like me, it went out again—and being no Daniel Boone you reached for some lighter fluid or gasoline and angrily soaked the whole pile. Again, if you are like me, you muttered to the men nearby not to tell your wife. Then you lit it again, and this time, it took.

It was a glorious thing to behold, and you stood there admiring it and enjoying the warmth. This was going to be a great fire. What a time you were going to have over the next few hours. Still, you knew better than to just walk away. The thing had to be tended, and you couldn't entrust this to anyone else.

The fire would burn for a while and everything would settle. Your wood would burn and weaken and your carefully crafted cathedral of logs would collapse. There were things you had to do. You couldn't leave the fire alone. Fires have to be messed with to be right. This is why God made pokers and tongs and bellows. So you rearranged and threw on more logs and then rearranged again. It all had to be just so.

If your friends are knuckleheads like mine, one of them threw half a cup of unwanted coffee on the fire. You had to fix this. Ashes had to be stirred, and you might have to blow on the coals to restore the damage. It would probably require another log.

In time, you would settle in. Human beings gathered around a fire are a beautiful thing to behold. People reflect and talk about life and even break into song. That is one of the main reasons you lit a fire in the first place.

Still, you stood watch. You had to make sure the children didn't get burned. You also had to watch every spark that took flight so it didn't set the woods on fire or light up the tiles on your roof. I can tell you from experience that letting a spark land on a dog will ruin the mood. That's about an hour of calling, cajoling, and comforting that you don't want to spend. Better to be on watch.

This is the art of it all, then. You've learned over time. If you want the sweetness of the gathering by the fire, you have to fight the low-grade battle to build and keep the flames leaping, the coals casting their glow. You are willing, though, because you want what a good fire brings to your life.

Fighting for the Flame

A poet with a sense of humor would call this the Battle of the Fire. I want to talk to you about another kind of battle that is somewhat the same. It is the Battle of Love. Now, I know this sounds like the title of a 1980s rock ballad, but I want you to take this approach to love seriously. For most men to keep the fire of love for their friends, their children, their wives, and even their God roaring, it makes all the difference if they think of it as being a battle. It summons the best from their souls, sounds the call to duty, and sets them on a grand adventure—which, of course, is exactly what love is.

There is a beautiful moment in the near-classic film *The Remains of the Day*, which is based on the eponymous Kazuo Ishiguro award-winning novel. It comes after the head butler of a stately British manor in the 1930s, a Mr. Stevens, allows his father to serve on the manor's staff. You can tell there is a stiff relationship between the two men. You can also tell something is bothering the older man. This goes on for quite a while. Eventually, the father's health fails. While he's on his death bed, he suddenly blurts out to his son, "I fell out of love with your mother." This, we are supposed to understand, is what is behind much of the distance and the undercurrent of resentment between the two men.

I think about this tender scene in the movie because I have often heard the same sentiment from older men. I spend most of my time with men of my age and younger but also make sure to spend time with men older than I am to enjoy their company and learn from their lives. I often ask them what they wish they had done better as men. What they tell me puts me right in that scene from *The Remains of the Day*. More than any other regret, older men have expressed to me that they wish they had known how to keep love alive.

Each of these conversations has marked me with their sad memories and air of remorse. These men have friends they lost because they let the flames of friendship—of manly love, really—die. They sit with a mystified look on their faces while they speak of wives they had lost all passion for. Marriages died. Hearts were pierced. Years were lost or torturous, and now they cannot remember why. They wished they could have it all back again.

Some have even spoken to me of estranged children, and I can feel the agony in the room. Still, something in them had just died toward their children, at least for a while, and they just let them drift away. What often strikes me is how these men lived otherwise successful, competent lives. Yet they lost the battle of love, and so from the vantage point of old age felt that none of their other victories were worth the price of what they lost in the lives of those they were supposed to love.

These conversations remind me of some others I've had. Because of my work I've had many debriefs with men about divorce, and many others with men about their affairs. Two truths emerged from these conversations that have stunned me but also cast light on this battle for love we must learn to fight.

First, the vast majority of men I've spoken to who have initiated divorces from their wives—not who had divorces visited upon them but who pursued the divorce themselves—have come to regret it. Eventually, they woke up and saw the beauty of what they once had. The second truth is that most men who have had affairs have lived to regret them also. One day they looked at the woman they chose over the woman they married and realized they made a mistake. Some men have even said to me, "I was actually in love with my wife. I just didn't know it. So I chose to mess around."

All of these reflections are confirmation of perhaps the most important truth we need to know. Love comes easily. It also drifts easily away. We have to fight to keep it and make it grow.

Think about those you love. You met that friend and it didn't take long before a manly friendship developed. In time, you would have used the word *love*. You probably can't even remember quite why you liked the guy so much, but you did. Friendship started. It grew. In time, love arrived.

It was even more of the same with your wife or the woman you love. You saw her. You were attracted. Perhaps she spoke and you melted. You spent time with her and found nearly everything she did endearing and as though it was what you had wanted all your life. There was little strain. Nothing about it was labor. You saw. You wanted. Love came.

Any man who has been there at the birth of his children has experienced much the same thing. Initially, they are just big round tummies that kick. You know there's a human in there but you can't really call what you feel love. Then they come out. Though they all look like Martians or Churchill when they do, you can't believe how you feel. They look at you. They coo. They smile, or maybe it's gas but you don't care. You lose your mind. You start acting ridiculous. They popped out. They're yours. Love came.

As sweet as all this is, we have to admit that these kinds of love can all go away. Friends grow apart. Husbands and wives divorce or perhaps live in loveless marriages. Parents and children can grow so distant they end up dying estranged. It is painful to admit but a quick gaze at the world as it is tells us it's true.

I would say that these things happen because we lose the battle for love, but the truth is that most of us never engage in the fight. We don't know there is one. We assume love will stay as effortlessly as it arrived. It usually doesn't. Love—for our friends, our children, our wives, and our God—has to be tended. It has to be protected and fed and repaired. It has to be fought for.

Now, this is not a book on relationships. This is no marriage manual or guide to parenting or handbook for having great friends. I strongly recommend all of these. Only a fool gets married but doesn't attend a good marriage conference or two with his wife, read some great books, and get help from friends. It is the same with children and friendships. Read and learn and study and ask questions. Get what you need as early as you can. It can all quite literally save your life.

This book, though, is about men and the fire in their gut. This chapter is about men fighting to keep love burning. So I want to describe some ways men can fight, some features of their souls that give them advantages in the battle for fiery love. This is going to be the shortest chapter of those on the seven fires but it may be the most hard-hitting. This is because I believe most men don't need to be talked to death. They simply need to be told how to uniquely fight as men in order to win and then get on with it.

Men and Vision

Men, let me give you some really bad news that has some good news in it. When aptitude tests are given to men and women, the results show that women are superior to men in every category except two. That's fine. Go ahead and grieve. It's true.

The two categories that men can call their own are abstract thought and aggression. Some men like to rename these *vision* and *drive*. Regardless of what we call them, we should give women their due and then get on with using our gifts for good.

It's the gift for vision that I most want to build on here. Thank God that men are usually equipped with a keen sense of vision. They can see what isn't there. They can envision what ought to come, perhaps what reality can ultimately be. This is what allows them to see in their mind's eye how the house should be remodeled or what that junky old car can one day become. They can envision a strategy for a game or imagine what their investments or degrees or labors should produce in twenty years. This gift is what helps them coach and build and lead and create. They have a vision of the ideal, the ultimate, the way things should be.

Now, men bring this gift to their relationships. When a man falls in love with a woman, for example, his gift for vision kicks in. He can imagine being with her all their days. He can envision the future, the house and the children and the trips and the dog and all the great times together—her at his side. He also usually has an overdone vision of her. She's not just Sally the art major from Topeka. She's Guinevere. She's a goddess. She's the most beautiful creature who ever lived.

112

This is all as it should be. The problem comes when reality sets in. Real life begins to happen. There are squabbles, letdowns, and failures to measure up. Over time, the woman or the friend or the children and even God don't match the vision in the man's head. A chip comes off the statue. The pristine image is tarnished and torn. This is when disappointment sets in for the man. This is when the progression begins with disillusionment, moves to resentment, and in turn becomes anger and a sense of betrayal. He's been tricked. He's been lied to. What is before him is far beneath the vision that once danced merrily in his head. And love starts to dim.

What a man must do to win the war for love is fight the battle for vision. He has to battle to keep a higher vision of those he loves living within him. He must become the Vision Keeper.

This is one of the great arts of manhood, and it plays into a man's innate gift for vision. He has to work to keep a loving, compassionate, tender view of his wife or his children or his friends constantly alive in his mind. If he doesn't, then he can begin to see everyone he knows as having failed him and then live out his life in bitterness and anger. You'll find many men like this camped out every day at the local bar, drowning their disillusionment.

These feelings are a possibility for all of us because everyone we know is flawed. They may have great gifts and beauty but they also have deformities, damage, and immaturities we just can't escape. If we focus on the negative, if we allow ourselves to be offended and put off by what we see, then we lose the things about them we love that caused us to attach to them in the first place. For a man to love well, he has to fight to hold tightly to a vision of the nobility and goodness of those in his life.

You've likely seen the same progression I have. A man loves a woman. He's crazy about her. He marries her. He feels at first like he's living in heaven on earth. Then the natural things of human life start happening. They have some conflicts. She gains some weight. She's late everywhere she goes. It turns out his wife doesn't cook as well as his mother does. There's also her frustrating loss of interest in sex. So the man thinks about these things all the time. He gripes to his friends. Other women begin to look awfully good to him. Why didn't he wait and marry one of them? He feels caught in a great marital bait and switch.

Now, to be a good man in a healthy marriage, he'll need to lovingly talk to his wife about his concerns. They'll need to work it out. Yet he won't do that if his heart is not still in the game, and his heart won't be in the game if he no longer sees the woman he married as his Guinevere, as a gift, as the most amazing woman he's ever known. She is all these things, but he has to keep them in focus—despite the sometimes disappointing realities of life settling in.

This is where a man's gift for vision serves him well. He has to battle to see her as she is at heart, apart from the weight and the last argument and the bad biscuits and the way he is losing her in bed. He has to fight for the vision of her that is true and inspiring. He has to remember how her words light him up and how she cradles a baby, and that sweet way she hums while she combs her hair. He has to feel a bit of her burden in putting up with him and see that she is fighting for a vision of him too. He has to do whatever it takes to remember the good and celebrate the sweet and keep all those amazing memories in view.

I know men who do this by making lists. One man creates photo albums on his computer that are filled with images of all the things he loves about his wife. A friend of mine even told his wife when he married her he was going to tell her every day something new he had fallen in love with about her. He's done it too, and that marriage— let me tell you—is on fire!

It's the same with our children. People will always disappoint. Your teenage son will not measure up every day to the vision you had for him when you were first told you had a son. Find the new vision. See him for who he is, apart from the chores that are undone and the job he lost and the C in math on his report card. He's a good kid with good things in him. Locate them. Be the Vision Keeper for his life. Don't smear over the gift that he is with your disappointment and disgust.

Every friend will require the same approach. Our buddies can be glorious to know but they also wound. They disappoint. Sometimes they just don't show up. It's easy to give up entirely on friendship. It's a battle for vision, though. It's a battle to keep who they are and what they've done and what they mean to you at their best in the center of your heart. Then you find the grace to walk out whatever comes.

Men and Forgiveness

It may surprise you to find that this gift men have for vision can also help us forgive. This is vital, because we men can destroy our lives with our failure to forgive. If you are like me, it is as though your soul is coated in Velcro and so offenses can easily attach and never let go. We have to find a way to get free, though, or we will live small, bitter, snarling, poisoned lives. We will taint every relationship we have.

I've seen the kind of men I don't want to be. They are older. They've sustained some wounds and let them fester. The toxins have seeped into their souls. Now, in their later years, they are bitter and hard. They can hardly carry on a conversation without spitting out their bile. They are angry at life and it shows. I often wonder, when I see men like this, what might have been different if they had only known how to peel offenses off of the Velcro of their souls. In fact, what if they had learned to remove the Velcro entirely? What might they be now, beyond the distant, snarling creatures they've become?

There are many guides and courses on forgiveness. I suggest you give them a look. We all need help in this all-important battle. Beyond these, though, I want to suggest a tactic in this battle that serves most men well and leans to their gift for vision.

Our tendency is to see those who've wronged us as simply evil. That coach who hammered you. The girl who betrayed you. The friends who shut you out. That client who cheated you. They are all wicked, you tend to believe. They are all just bad people. In their evil they wronged you, and that's where it stops. It was a case of evil versus innocence, pure and simple. The problem is, as long as you believe this you can never forgive.

The tactic that changes this is the hook of compassion. If you can think about those who wronged you and find some compassionate insight, some glimmer of understanding for why they did what they did, then you may find the power to let the offense go. You'll free yourself. You'll free others. In your closer relationships, you'll be fighting the battle for love.

It may be that the coach hammered you because that was the only coaching style he knew. He had been cussed out and criticized by his father and by his own coaches. He took it as love. He thought it was what you do when you believe in a guy. It wasn't personal. Perhaps you can let it go. That girl who betrayed you may have fled the relationship because she thought you were about to dump her. Those friends didn't mean to shut you out. Maybe they thought you didn't like them much. And so it goes. There are reasons people do what they do. It is not all about them hating you. Perhaps you can find, with your gift for vision, some understanding of what made them behave as they did.

Then, perhaps, you can let it go. The lack of forgiveness you feel toward your wife is killing your love. It's the same with your children and friends. You've got to engage in the battle to forgive. Unforgiveness is a cancer to love, and you've got to drive it out of your soul. Otherwise, love dims. Then it flees. Then we become old men regretting how we let love die in our lives.

There's a battle to fight. It's a battle for vision. Engage in it and win.

The Power of Habits

There is a third tactic that men can use in the battle for a fiery love. It comes from one of the great gifts men have: to give themselves to habits.

I love the way that repeated physical experiences can reset emotions in men. It is a gift. If a man wears a hard hat every day at work, just putting on that hard hat can reset his entire state of mind for work. He's conditioned himself. His whole being responds. I have a doctor friend who says no matter what mood he is in when he arrives at his office, when he puts the lab coat on and the stethoscope around his neck, this simple act aligns his whole being for work. It is this way with most men.

I have my own experience of this. I play racquetball. I've held a racquet in my hand for thousands of hours in my life. No matter where I am, if I pick up my racquet—even in my living room—and strap it on and hold it like I do when I play, then my whole body starts preparing to play. This is merely the power we have to condition ourselves through repeated physical experiences.

It is the same when it comes to loving someone. For a man, the deeds of love can help condition the soul for love. Actions help to create conditions of the heart. We should use this in the battle for loving people.

I have experienced this in a discipline my father taught me. He nearly always opened the car door for my mother. He taught me to do the same. Now it is a habit. I nearly always open the car door for my wife. She is certainly capable of doing it herself. Yet it is what a man does—to show honor, to show care, to protect, to serve, and to reveal tenderness. Old school, I know, but I believe in it fully.

Here's what I want you to know. When I start walking toward the car to open the door for my wife, all the things I've just described come up in my heart. I've opened her door thousands of times in our years, I'm sure. Each time, the deed summons the feelings. The doing surfaces the condition of the heart. I've even started to believe that

I should open my wife's car door more for my sake than for hers, because the doing draws out affection and tenderness and honor that are there but not active when I'm going about my normal day.

The principle is that habits of honor surface honor. Habits of love surface love. Habits of tenderness surface tenderness. This is the way a man is made, and it can help him in his battle for loving well.

So one of the arts of manly loving is that we build in habits for those we love. We routinely touch. We set regular time for telling the kids stories. We wrestle every Saturday morning. We have date nights. We make a habit of small gifts. We learn a thing or two about massage and make it a regular gift. There are a million ways to do this. Each man should find his own.

I know one guy who, along with all the other habits he built in, simply made the bed. His wife went to work every day before him. He made the bed when he got up. It became a habit. Once he did this regularly, he then couldn't leave a sink of dishes behind. He'd begun to care about what his wife found when she got home. This went even further. He started doing a bit of sprucing around the house before he left in the morning. He also started preparing a little tray for her each day to find when she got home. It only took a few minutes. He'd put a bit of wine and some nuts and perhaps a satchel of bath salts on a tray with a note. Imagine how that felt to her each day when she came in. I know—the dude makes us all look bad. He and his wife are crazy for each other, though. Manly loving habits are one of the main reasons why.

The Battle over Ourselves

Now, gentlemen, a final word. There is another way in which we need to deploy our vision abilities in battling for love. This is in the battle over ourselves.

To love well, we have to be willing to change often. We have this in us. We know how to adapt, to learn, to retool in order to get jobs done. It is the same when we love people. We want to hold on to the core of who we are, but we also should understand that love means constantly contending with ourselves to be better men.

If a man grows up in a hard-talking, sarcastic family, it shapes him. Later, he falls in love with a woman. He wants to give her a beautiful life. Yet she is a tender soul, and she hurts every time he's harsh with his words. Love means he has to change.

What does he do? He has to get a vision. He has to see himself as a gentler man. He has to watch other men who are kind in their manner and use words to build and not to harm. He has to develop a vocabulary of tender terms and cut out the locker room banter he's used to—at least at home. It is pretty much the same process he used when he learned how to swing a bat or play guitar or dress for a date. He watched those who did it well. He learned. He did likewise. What happened? He got a vision of what it would look like when he did it right. Then he made the needed changes.

Love means you study your wife and children and friends. You listen. What are they asking of you? What doesn't work? What about you is getting in the way? Don't be offended. All they are signaling is that they want more of you without stuff you've accumulated getting in the way. Get a vision of yourself as you should be. You can drop weight. You can serve. You can be a bit more romantic. You can turn off the TV and get rowdy with the kids. You can be a better dresser or learn some technique in bed or master that anger problem with the help of God and some friends. None of this erases who you are. Get a vision. Live it out. Be a loving man.

Let's take this home by recalling where we began. In the same way a man tends a fire, love requires tending too. Love may come easily into our lives, but it leaves easily too. If you want love to stay and deepen, you have to tend it. You have to protect it. You have to adapt. You have to walk out a manly vision of a loving man.

You can do it. God has already put the needed equipment in your soul. No man loses the love in his life because he just can't love. More often, he just doesn't know how to fight for it. He doesn't know how to tend it. He doesn't know how to build a fire that will remain.

Trust God. Trust your band of brothers. Get a vision for loving manhood and walk it out. It will bring great riches to your life.

THE BATTLE PLAN

1. Ponder the examples of manly love you've had in your life. What parts of this example would you want to build upon? What do you want to avoid? Be specific about this and take notes if it will help you keep focus.

2. Pull your band of brothers together and talk about this matter of vision. When in your life have you had a vision and made it a reality? What did you do that made it work? Identify the steps if you can. Ask your men to tell you how this gift for vision has worked for their good in their lives.

3. List the people you want to love well. Have you dimmed in your affection for them, or do you have a clear, loving vision of who they are? If you've dimmed a bit, start refocusing your vison. Find the good and noble things about them. Work these into a way of seeing these people you want to love well. Get your friends to hold you accountable for keeping this vision at the center of your focus. Grow this over time with new perspectives and experiences that draw out affection toward them.

4. Be courageous and honest enough to make a list of people you know you need to forgive. Try to find the hook of compassion for the things they did that offended you. You will need help from your band of brothers for this. They will have perspective you don't have. Once you find the hook of compassion, do the inner work to let your offense go. If these

people can be reached and they know about your problem with them, contact them and make it right.

5. With your band of brothers, recall honestly the traits you have been challenged to change in yourself. Ask for perspective from your men. Make the changes you know you need to make. Get help. Get input. Have your men hold you accountable. Take it one change at a time but give it your best. Ask the men around you who can coach you in the specific changes you need to make to love well.

6. Do a loving habits inventory. What are you doing now? What do those you love need? How can you build manly loving habits in your life? Ask your men to tell you of their experiences in this. Start building what you learn into your life without fanfare or announcements to those you love. Let your deeds speak for themselves. Only do as much of this as you can do consistently, lovingly, and well.

6

The Fire of Legacy

What you leave behind is not what is engraved in stone monuments, but what is woven into the lives of others.

Pericles[1]

When I was doing graduate work in history, I came across two stories that stirred me about the power of what passes through generations. I want to tell you those stories now as we ponder this matter of men and legacy.

The first story is about a sailor who lived in the early 1300s. During his many years at sea, this man once served on a boat that was sailing near the coast of North Africa. One day his captain made the decision to take a dying man on board. The man's name was Lully, and he was a missionary in Tunis. Only days before, a mob had stoned him nearly to death. It was obvious he would not survive, and this is why our sailor's captain decided to have mercy and care for the dying man.

It would be a fairly unremarkable story except that before this man died, he said something to the crew that our sailor never forgot.

From his death bed, the missionary pointed west across the Atlantic Ocean and said that beyond those vast waters there was another continent that was largely unknown. He said his hearers should send men there to save souls. Then he died.

The moment made an impression on our lone sailor. When he returned home, he told his family of that missionary and his amazing words. This sailor's sons told their sons, and these grandsons in turn told their sons. And so it went in that family for more than a century and a half.

Finally, a young boy in that family line sat at his father's knee and heard the tale of the dying missionary and an unknown continent and an urgent plea to save souls. Each time the boy heard this story, he felt it stirring something within him. It awakened his curiosity. It began to haunt his imagination. He later decided to investigate the possibility that there was an inhabited continent across the great sea.

This boy's name was Christoforo Columbo. You know him better as Christopher Columbus.[2] What you may not know is that part of what caused him to think that a voyage west from Europe might reach a new continent was a story that had been passed down through his family line. It had become part of the legacy given him by his ancestors. It also became, in time, a commission to fulfill.

The second story that brought the immensity of legacy before my eyes was actually a single fact that carried a thousand stories with it. I was reading a book about the Middle Ages written by the eminent historian William Manchester. In his description of the great Canterbury Cathedral in England, he included these few words: "Canterbury was twenty-three generations in the making."[3]

I remember thinking about this fact for hours. Twenty-three generations. I dug deeper into it, and what I learned inflamed my historical imagination. It seems that there were men who worked nearly all their lives on a single section of the great cathedral. Their sons apprenticed under them and knew that they in turn would also make the immense structure their life's work. They were eager to do it. It was work for the glory of God. It was a cathedral that would last for centuries. They would enlist their sons in this meaningful venture, and through them the generations afterward.

We know that men passed their skills and their tools on to the next generation. Occasionally this would happen in brief ceremonies. Picture it. An elderly man on a stretcher, living his last days, asks to be carried to the portion of the great building where he has labored all his life. He gazes admiringly at what he has done. He speaks to his sons and grandsons about pride in their craft and the commission they must fulfill. He has already passed most of his tools to them. Now he gives one final symbolic tool, perhaps a cherished chisel or an instrument he has invented himself, to each of his sons. He is done. It is their calling now.

For twenty-three generations this was done. Men sometimes labored within several yards of the work of their great-grandfathers. They used their fathers' tools. They completed what had been started before they were born. In some cases, they labored knowing that the cathedral would not be finished for centuries.

I remember that these two tales from history reached places deep within me when I first read them. Perhaps they do the same for you. The reason, I suppose, is that we men are made to live lives that echo not only in eternity but also in the generations that follow us. We are meant to understand ourselves as part of a march through time. As we should receive a heritage from our fathers and mothers, so we should pass a legacy on to our sons and daughters. We are not meant to be about one generation. We are not meant to be about only our time. We are meant to launch those entrusted to us further than we ourselves can go.

We often hear such sentiments discussed among men, and it can all take on a sense of vanity and self-exaltation. We want to "make our mark." We want our name to be remembered. We want to be thought great and exemplary. So we hope to have our name on a university building one day, or we want the business we founded to last a century, or we hope something we do will be mentioned in the history books. Each of these aspirations is fine, as long as we do not neglect the more important matters of leaving a legacy by being good men, by providing for those who follow us, and by passing on the culture of valiant manhood so it can last for generations in our family line.

In my work with men I am often deeply moved when they speak to me of their hopes for their sons and daughters. Often these men have some simple object that has passed down through their family line. I've sat with men who held pocketknives their fathers had given them or tools or books or in one case even a razor. With tears in their eyes they've told me of the day they envision giving these things to their sons and commissioning them, as it were, to authentic manhood. Several of these men said they hoped they were worthy of their sons in the examples they set and the lessons they taught by how they lived. Imagine this. A man hoping to live worthy of the potential of his son. Beautiful.

I am inspired by all such passions in men, in part because they are rare today. We live at a time when personal pleasure and profit are the goal of most men, with very little attention given to all who will follow us. However, this generational myopia is nothing new.

Men and the Next Generation

In a story from the ancient world, there was once a king who welcomed envoys from a rival people to his kingdom. He showed them all that was in his treasury and all the immense wealth in his storehouses. There was nothing in his palace or kingdom that he did not reveal.

When these envoys left, a wise man came to him and asked him about what he had done. After the king told him, the wise man said, "Here is what is going to happen now. Everything you have and all that you have worked to build is going to be carried off by the armies of these foreigners. Nothing will be left. Also, your descendants, your own flesh and blood, will be taken away. Your sons are going to be eunuchs in the house of this foreign king. Your daughters are going to be the playthings of your enemies."

It was a devastating prophecy. Oddly, the king seemed to take it well. "What you have said is good," he replied, probably trying to sidestep the horrible thing he had done with a compliment to the wise man. Yet we are also told in this ancient tale what the king was thinking as he said these words: "Will there not be peace and security in my lifetime?" (2 Kings 20:12–19).

There it is. Almost the creed of our age. *I'm not worried by what comes after I'm gone. After all, I'll enjoy peace and security in my lifetime.*

This attitude is a cancer on our time. It is also a cancer on great manhood in our generation. It is a kind of bigotry, the disregard of an entire people out of a preoccupation with ourselves. When the experts tell us that the lives of the young are not likely to be of the same quality as the lives of their parents, this attitude is why. When one generation runs up massive debts that the next generation has to pay, this "I'll have peace and safety in my lifetime" thinking is the reason. When one generation destroys the environment or corrupts its politics or refuses to face social crises and thus leaves a mess to the next generation, this idolatrous selfishness is the cause.

I sometimes see in men this disregard of legacy in very practical ways. I'm often stunned to find when a man dies that he has made no provision for his wife or his children. I've often been part of the teams left to work with devastated widows and damaged children who have been left nothing but debt and legal quagmires by a supposedly loving man. I know of a high-ranking military officer who died in retirement and yet left no life insurance policy, no property, and no savings to his longsuffering wife. I know of a musician who left only debt to his. All this is the product of an attitude, a spirit, a grinding self-absorption that leaves no room for concern about the future suffering of others.

This contempt for what comes after us in our families is much the same as a cultural contempt for the well-being of the next generation. Every generation should see itself as entrusted with the care of those who will follow us. The well-being of the young after we are gone is part of the duty and the joy of our generation.

The Fuel of Legacy

I've been speaking in almost financial terms about this matter of legacy, but of course I believe it is far more than that. Leave wealth to your descendants if you can. Leave at least an insurance policy. Most every man can do this much. Yet it is what we leave of ourselves in the lives of those who follow us that is the true legacy. Men are incomplete without this fire burning within them.

Many of the achievements of great men and great eras of men were fueled by a desire to protect the next generation and set it on its course. There were inventors who said they did what they did to remove a blight from the lives of their children's children. War heroes said that what was in their minds as they did their heroic deeds was keeping their children free. Mighty social reformers were thinking largely of people still unborn when they combated poverty or attacked ignorance or worked for civil rights. The World War II generation in Britain arose magnificently largely to keep future generations from having to be Nazis. Pilgrims sailed to a new world and pioneers tamed frontiers and settlers harnessed the wilderness almost always with those who would follow them in mind.

This is what men do. This is how men think when they are at their best. This is one of the motivating forces that is meant to burn in a man's soul and make him greater than he would be if only serving himself. It is a duty and something of a burden, yes, but it is also part of what makes a man a true man and what unleashes powerful forces in his soul.

It is important to say also that this matter of legacy is not merely a matter for men with children. It is a matter for men with heart. Some of the finest men I know are single and have no intention of having children should they marry, but they think about the good of future generations nearly every day. I know sixteen-year-olds who are years from marriage but have already determined to be models for the young and protectors of their future good. You should see the masculine strength and nobility this determination draws from their souls. A man can care about the young, he can care about tomorrow, he can care about a generation still unborn without having a wife or children of his own. In fact, this is precisely the point. Legacy is not about us and our condition. It is about what we impart to those who follow us. Doing this well is one of the great arts of manhood.

So, how does a man leave a legacy? How does he prepare to make the imprint he is called to make upon the next generation?

Memento Mori

Leaving a legacy begins with the way a man defines his life, and I believe this is best done by contemplating death. Throughout history, people have believed that they would live richer, more meaningful lives if they would contemplate their deaths. What would they want to be on the day of their deaths? What would they want to have achieved? What would they hope to have written on the hearts of those they love? What would they hope to have created that they can hand to those who follow them?

This is the reason you see skulls built into the architecture of European cathedrals. They are not there to symbolize evil but rather to remind us to contemplate death. Writers of earlier generations signed letters with the Latin phrase *memento mori*. It means simply "remember death." The assumption was that people would live more fruitful lives if they would think about their end. This is what Winston Churchill was getting at when he wrote, "When the tones of life ring false, we should refer to the tuning fork of death."[4] It is also what the writer of Ecclesiastes meant when he penned, "Death is the destiny of everyone; the living should take this to heart" (Eccles. 7:2).

If we look at the whole of our lives from now until our death and view it all through the lens of what we are meant to leave to the next generation, this will start to redefine the way we live. We'll be kept from thinking only in terms of our wants and needs and will start building a plan for those who come after us.

This is the key. We stop thinking about our lives as being our own. We start believing that our lives, in part, belong to those still to come. We build a generational plan into all we do, from how we run our businesses to how we father, from how we set an example by how we live to how we design our wills. We understand that our lives upon our deaths will not be deemed righteous by God and humanity without the good of the next generation being assured as far as we can.

In short, we have to redefine what it means to be men. A man doesn't conquer and build for himself. He doesn't use everyone in his life for his own selfish purposes. He doesn't seek peace and safety in his lifetime and scoff at whatever comes to those after him. He has to believe that his life is measured in part by how he impacts the next generation. This is the will of God. This is the call on his life. This is the plea of his children. This is the definition of what it means to be a man.

The Daily Imprint of Legacy

So we begin by redefining manly life. Then we have to get practical. We build a legacy not just with huge matters of wills and property. We do it with the daily things. We do it by writing every day on the lives around us. We intentionally imprint the souls of those entrusted to us.

Here is a principle I hope you will never forget: you build a legacy by investing in others. Most men define *legacy* in terms of themselves, of what their name will be written upon and how their memory will endure. A good man's legacy, though, is written on lives and endures not primarily through institutions and financial instruments but through the honor given him by those he has shaped.

So it is this matter of investing in others that we ought to be about. It means, first, that we have to think about them. This seems almost silly to mention, but we are often so busy that we fail to ponder the lives and needs of those entrusted to us. What imprint does your daughter need from your life? What impartation does your son need? How can the men around you feed from your life in such a way that it makes them better men?

These are not questions about the short term, either. We have to zoom out from the immediate and ask what vast imprint we ought to be making before the next generation is sent off into their lives. What of the higher values—nobility, honor, service, sacrifice, faith, courage, leadership—do we have that we can plant in the soil of the next generation?

I have a friend who has taken this very seriously. He does something I would recommend to all men intent upon leaving a legacy. He has what he calls a legacy plan for each of his children and others whom he feels called to impact. It is an actual written plan for each one. He has shown it to me, and it is an inspiring thing to behold.

One of his children, a son, is named Shawn. My friend thought about this son, took stock of his gifts and his weaknesses, and paid attention to the tendencies of his soul and his manner out in the world. My friend quickly saw his son's aptitude for science. He makes sure he feeds this gift with everything he can: trips, reading, and discussion. If a leading scientist is speaking at the nearby university, my friend and his son are there. He's also saving for the scientific education he knows is coming. He's constantly feeding his son's gift without being pushy.

And by thinking deeply about his son, my friend also detected an enemy that might ruin Shawn's life. He realized that the boy had a tendency toward fear and cowardice. The young man was so brilliant that he was always able to figure out the ninety things that might go wrong with anything he did. This made him hesitant, uncertain, and haunted by the thought of danger.

My friend's legacy plan included answering this challenge. Some years ago he set out to add to Shawn's stunning intelligence the soul of a courageous, confident man. He started talking to his son about his own fears and how he overcame them. He has gone on adventures with the boy—hunting, learning to scuba dive, and even serving the impoverished in tough parts of the world. He has put him with men of adventure and sometimes drew the kid into pickup football games where he got knocked around and bloodied but had a ball. Always there is the debrief. Always there is the discussion about how it felt to face fear and overcome it. Always there is the celebration of victories won. Shawn began realizing that dangers loomed but they could be bested. Wounds happened but they didn't last. He also began living a thrilling life. All of this has changed him.

Shawn's mother tells the story best. She says that the child who once snuck away from school at the end of the day because he was afraid of the other kids eventually became the bold young man excitedly talking about how he had seen sharks when he was sixty feet down on an ocean dive. The same kid who used to hide in his books to avoid anything unsettling started throwing himself into martial arts, looking forward to the next hunting trip with Dad, and planning to run the bulls in Pamplona, Spain, right after his graduation from high school.

How had it happened? My friend stepped enough into his son's life that the boy could drink from his spirit. He saw the beauty of a hunt through his dad's eyes. He saw his father get knocked down hard in a touch football game and get up laughing. He felt his father's thrill at facing dangers and transcending them. In other words, my friend offered a manly, courageous spirit to his son, and the young man took that spirit to heart. Dad's courageous legacy is forever imprinted on his son's soul.

Now, this might sound like a father's relatively short-term corrective work with a teenage son. It is so much more. Think of what it will mean through the years. Think of how Shawn will storm into adversity, master challenges, defy danger, and give himself to a brave and accomplished life because his father invested in him. This will live in Shawn long after his father is dead. He will tell the story to others. He will impart his spirit to the people around him. Lives will be changed.

Now this, gentlemen, is a legacy.

Narrating the World

Another tactic men use in leaving a legacy is to constantly narrate the world around them in manly terms for their children. I also see men doing this who have no children but who hope to impact the young. This brings me to one of the biggest challenges I want to issue in this book.

Many of us were raised by men who were admirable in their character but who rarely spoke. They were typical of their generation. They did what they did and expected that their deeds would speak for themselves. They did not explain. They did not narrate. You were expected to notice and understand.

I was raised by such a man. My father, as I've said, set an example of duty, honor, and heroism. He was a good man who led a life of sacrifice for his country and his family. Still, I mean no disrespect when I tell you that he never explained anything to me as a man. He never said, "Here is what a man does." He never said, "Son, men don't do things that way." He explained almost nothing unless I had done something wrong, and then he "explained" in ways that made distinct impressions on my mind and body. As a result, I was left to figure things out on my own or seek out mentors, which I've spent a lifetime doing. I love my father, but I learned almost nothing from him that did not come from quietly watching.

This has barely worked for men of my age. It will not work for the young today. We live in a highly verbal, media-oriented world. Ideas come at the young too fast for them to digest it all on their own. If the older generation delays in explaining the world or parents are cowardly in dealing with difficult things, then the world will explain itself to the young, and we won't be happy with the results.

If we want to fashion a legacy in the souls of the young, we have to get there early and get there with a better narrative. We have to explain the world well and preemptively. Men, hear me. You can't wait to explain sex to a young man until he is already dating. Can you imagine when a boy in our world first sees a photo of a naked woman? It is far earlier than most men would ever imagine. Too early. You have to get there first. You have to explain well. You have to mentor. It is the same with violence, drugs, stealing, or any of a hundred other things young men are tempted to do. You have to beat the world to the punch in narrating reality for the young. We can't claim the excuse that women are better at such things. We need to step manfully into the lives of our sons and daughters and frame the world for them in righteous, moral, inspiring, and fearless but wise terms.

I'm listing dark and perhaps troubling things here. This is because what excites me most is what men can achieve in the lives of those around them when they simply explain manliness in relatable, casual, meaningful terms. I've watched a particular father I know who brings "what men do" into nearly everything he explains to his children. They ask why he's working out. He doesn't just give them a biological explanation. He says that a good man keeps himself healthy so he can love his wife and care for his children. He wants to be strong to serve around the house. He wants to be able to protect his family. He wants to live long and love his grandchildren and maybe his great-grandchildren. This is what good men do, and he wants to be one of them.

I know another man whose young daughter asked him why he was working so hard on the family's financial records. Now, some men would say, "Because you guys cost so dang much! We spend too much around here and I'm tired of having to hack away at a budget no one pays any attention to!" This approach only smears the whole topic with anger and resentment. My friend does exactly the opposite. When asked, he said, "You know, this is one of the things I get to do because I'm your father. A man cares for his family. He earns. He makes sure his children have what they need. That's why your mother and I work and then make very careful plans like what I'm looking over now. It thrills me to know you guys are going to always be taken care of while you live with us. This is part of my privilege as a man." Can you imagine what arises in the heart of this man's children? Pure joy. Pure gratitude. Pure excitement about fulfilling manly and womanly duties themselves when the time comes.

This is one of the great arts of manhood. We narrate the world not just in natural and process terms. We narrate it in terms of the manhood we want to imprint on the next generation. We talk about everything fearlessly. We let the young know there is nothing they can't bring up, nothing that will rattle or upset us. When we answer, we frame the world they are going to live in. We set the stage for their lives. We precondition their souls to live noble lives.

This is best done when manly thoughts fall from us in small amounts as we live our lives before the young. I remember watching the news with my grandfather one evening when a politician began speaking. My grandfather huffed and said, "Now, if this fella was any kind of man, he would just tell the truth and put all this behind him." This was decades ago. I remember it to this day, and it shaped my understanding of manhood. At another time, my mother read a newspaper story out loud and then said to all of us children, "That's just not the way a man conducts himself. This guy is missing something on the inside. Real men would never let this happen." I listened. I remembered. It shaped me. My grandfather and mother are long gone, but you are reading about their words because they form part of a legacy that graces my life.

A final thought on this. It is intriguing that when the ancients spoke of the elder teaching the younger, they nearly always spoke of it happening "on the way." They meant while stuff is happening, while you're doing things with them. When I say narrate the world to the young and do it in terms of righteous manhood, don't picture a classroom. Don't picture a living room full of kids sitting at attention waiting for the start of the lecture. Teach as you do. Frame while in motion. Narrate while on the move. At the store, on the trip, over dinner, during the project, after the trouble at school. Think of your own life in this regard. You probably hardly remember the "sit-down lectures" you got from your parents. You probably remember well what your father taught you while you built a shed or fished or went on that trip. Build a legacy "on the way." It is what men do.

The Importance of Ritual

A third tactic for building an inner legacy in the lives around you is ritual. We tend to think of ritual as outdated, dead tradition in our day, but living rituals is one of the best ways to embed meaning and create a legacy in human hearts. They are also, frankly, an easier way to impart meaning than constantly crafting new experiences.

Let me offer two examples from my own life. My children have the misfortune of having a man who loves history as their father. This love gave me knowledge of one of the great rituals that has come down to us from those we call our Pilgrim Fathers in my country. I learned that when they sailed to the New World on the *Mayflower* and arrived in 1620, they were not prepared for the hardships they would endure. They suffered a horrible "starving time." Rations got down to five kernels of corn a day and some brackish water. It was ghastly. In time, things changed. Farming methods improved due to help from their native friends, and the Pilgrims were able to grow enough to meet all their needs. This abundance allowed them to celebrate a Thanksgiving Day.

Later generations of New Englanders did not want to forget the sufferings of their forebears, so they developed the tradition of putting five kernels of corn on every plate at the Thanksgiving meal. Before the great feast was eaten, people looked at those five kernels of corn on those otherwise empty plates, remembered the starving time at Plymouth, and said a prayer of thanksgiving for deliverance and grace. It is a beautiful ritual that survives to this day.

It also survived in the Mansfield home. Each year, before the eating began, I made sure that five kernels of corn were placed on each plate. Then I briefly told the story of the Pilgrims and we prayed. When my children were young, they competed to put the corn on the plates and to say the prayer. They even corrected me if I misstated some detail of the Thanksgiving story that they knew by heart. As they got older, they rolled their eyes while Dad droned on about people who lived four long centuries ago. How boring!

Today, though, my children will mention this tradition at Thanksgiving and get irritated with me if I talk of laying it aside. My daughter assures me that her children will help with the corn and know the story. "It's tradition, Dad! I won't ever lose it." So into the next generation will go a story that not only means a great deal to me but is also part of a heritage of faith and heroism, of hardship and ingenuity. This ritual, then, helped fashion part of the legacy I'm leaving to those who survive me.

I learned the power of such things from my parents, and this brings me to my second story. My father was, as I've said, a good man but not one for religion. Many a Sunday our home looked like the famous Norman Rockwell painting of the mother and children snootily heading off for church while Dad stays behind, hunkered down in his bathrobe with the newspaper.

Yet every Christmas, the situation would change. Dad was sentimental about Christmas and gave himself to it. On Christmas Eve, he morphed. He was happy. He cooked for us all. He taunted the kids about whether they had been good enough the previous year for Santa Claus to come to our house. Then, late in the evening, while we kids crammed sweets into our mouths and Mother looked on, Dad would read the story of the birth of Jesus from the Bible.

It was a simple thing but it profoundly impacted all of us. To hear the Bible in our father's voice and at such a moment was an experience that shaped us to this day. I can still hear the words in my memory. I still have the sense of the sacred from those nights, and still credit those moments for drawing me to God as a man.

You would have waited in vain for my father to preach. You might have been disappointed had you merely asked him to pray at a meal. Yet a gentle ritual embedded in love and generosity on a holy night changed my life more than if my father had lectured me about faith every day. This is the power of ritual.

We can build these moments into our lives in a thousand ways. There are meal rituals and sports rituals and the things we sing and what we talk about when we're on a trip. There are the traditions of symbolic gifts and the traditions of simple phone calls at precise times and sweet little ceremonies that can surround all the transitions of life. There is a manly art to elevating these moments from being merely about the food or the gathering or the gift to being about words that affirm and call out, about something that elevates and will endure.

This is what simple rituals can do, and they are possible with everyone in a man's life, particularly those who will carry his imprint after he is gone. Rituals build a legacy, and the wise man constructs them strategically throughout his life.

So, what have we seen? Define your life to include your calling to shape the next generation. Invest in those entrusted to you. Narrate the world for the young as you live. Use ritual to embed righteous forces in those who will follow you.

I believe in all of these things. I practice them. I've heard men attest to the impact of these manly tactics for decades. Yet I want to tell you the one thing that I've heard most described as the way men fashion a legacy.

The Power of Manly Example

There is simply no question that the greatest way for a man to leave a legacy is by example. It is by how he lives, particularly in moments of crisis. It is what his children and those around him see in his life.

Let me use a negative example first. It is a harsh one, I warn you. It is what happens in a family when a parent or grandparent commits suicide. Now I want to treat this in the most gracious way possible, but I cannot step away from acknowledging the tainting of a family when this sad thing happens.

I have known families that had everything going for them. They were wealthy and well-known. Nearly everyone had degrees from fine schools. They had everything people of our time seem to want: houses and cars, careers and awards, even bright shiny teeth. Yet if one parent or grandparent committed suicide, this horrible thing outshone all else. It was the label that stuck the longest. It was the banner over the family name. Of course, the pain would diminish over time and the goodness would return. Yet the point is that all of the wealth and fame and good looks and success in the world will not silence the echo of a negative example in a family line. It bleeds into the next generation. It has to be intentionally cleansed over time.

I share this dark thing about families to highlight the positive. In the same way horrible deeds cast shadows on family lines, noble deeds cast a brilliant and ennobling light. Here is the lesson: Character rules. Character redeems. Character lives on.

What the next generation sees in you of virtues such as courage, devotion, honesty, sacrifice, and faith is what will burn in their hearts long after you are gone. We say often that "more is caught than is taught." In other words, people receive more from our deeds than our words. It is the same with a legacy. More is observed than is given. More is absorbed from an example of character than is written into a check.

I wish as I write these words that I could replay for you all the stories I have heard about men who shaped powerful legacies through character. There are the dramatic ones. I know of a father who died stepping in front of a car to save his wife while their children looked on. It was obviously devastating to that family, but his example and sacrifice has built a family legacy of courageous, generous adults who have made a huge impact on the world. Their father's name is on their lips nearly every day.

There are also the gritty stories. A friend's father was a drug addict and a pimp. The man was an embarrassment to his family. He was constantly in and out of jail. Yet one day this father secretly watched his young son play basketball. The boy wasn't much good at it, but his father saw the young man's heart and realized how he needed a righteous man in his life. In a move that stunned everyone who knew him, this drug addict father got cleaned up. He broke his addiction, addressed his criminal past, and started earning a place in his son's life. It is one of the greatest second acts I've ever heard about. My friend is now a highly accomplished man. His father was at his side nearly every day after that basketball game until the moment he died. The legacy lives on in grandchildren and great-grandchildren and in foundations in this exemplary father's name.

There are also less visible examples. I know of a man whose business partner secretly cheated clients and cheated on the firm's taxes. It was a humiliating experience that nearly impoverished his family. Yet this man paid back every dime, though it took years, and rebuilt far more than was lost. His seven children saw it all. They are people of ethics and hard work and gratitude because of the legacy they have received.

I also have a friend whose father was a missionary. The man was treated horribly by his denomination time and again. Yet he kept his faith, kept his joy, and touched thousands of lives in his work. His children were at his side and drank deeply from his spirit. You could not know happier, funnier, more giving, gracious people than his descendants. Yet they might have been tainted by bitterness and grief.

This is what it means for a man to build a legacy through examples of character. How does he speak? What does he love? Who does he honor? Where does he sacrifice? How does he own up to his obligations? How does he give himself to a cause? Can he be tender and kind? These are the things that are remembered most and that shape the next generation the deepest.

These, then, are the manly tactics of legacy building. Yet before I bring this chapter to a close, let me offer a strong warning about the kind of legacy that is a ticking time bomb in a family line, a destroyer of honor and good.

A Warning about Bitterness

Many families have suffered wrongs, both in previous generations and among those alive today. There are racial injustices and hard things visited by criminal deeds and social wrongs that can wound beyond describing. There are devastations that come from wicked employers and horrors that beset good people from the darkest urges of humanity. Life can hurt. People can do harm. No one is immune.

The challenge for every man who wants to build a legacy is to combat the bitterness that these hard things of life can embed in a family line. We want to be honest about our history. We want to lay blame where it is due. Yet we cannot sit at dinner tables year after year and rehearse the wrongs done to us with rancor without passing a corroding force on to the next generation. We must do something to clean up the stream flowing into those who come after us. We must filter the sewage. We must somehow free ourselves of bitterness and pass a redemptive vision into the future.

Bitterness is a cancer. It is poison. However justified our feelings of resentment, they ruin us if they rule us. They make us small and angry, snarling and weak. A wise man once said that bitterness is like drinking poison thinking the other person will die. It may feel good to us for a season, but as a way of life it only destroys. Passed to the next generation, it can pummel to dust all the nobler facets of a legacy.

What can be done? I had the privilege of writing a book about Booker T. Washington. I knew before I started this book that he was a great man. He had founded Tuskegee Institute in Alabama, preached a message of uplift that changed his people, was the first man of his skin color to dine in the White House, and was, in his day, the most famous black man in the world. I admire him deeply.

Yet it was what I came to understand about his attitude toward slavery that first astonished me and then helped me deal with forgiveness in my own life. You see, Booker T. Washington was born a slave. We still have the record of a census that was taken when he was only four years old. It says, simply, "1 negro boy—$400." Imagine being valued in such a way. Imagine knowing all your life that you were once merely property with a price tag around your neck.

This was Booker T. Washington. He was born in a dirt-floor shack, abandoned by his father, raised by his overworked mother, and despised like millions of others for the color of his skin. He had to endure the humiliations the post–Civil War years visited upon blacks and all the horrors that befell his race in his time.

I read his life story and wondered that he did not give his life to bitter revenge. I think I might have. Slavery was a holocaust for his people, and it was hard to believe that a black man could ever rise above it. But Booker T. Washington did.

We should remember that he was a Christian, a man who believed in a sovereign God who could cause all things to work for the good of his people. For Washington, this meant a higher understanding of slavery. He believed that in the hands of God, the experience of slavery could make his people better. He did not deny the evil of the entire system or apologize for the vile souls who made it a way of life, but he did believe it could be turned to good for black Americans.

He stunned whites and blacks alike by speaking of "the school of American slavery" as a "wilderness through which and out of which a good providence has already led us."[5] He believed that in the hands of God, the black man had taken more out of slavery than slavery had ever taken out of him. He insisted that after the years of slavery, blacks were "in a stronger and more hopeful condition, materially, intellectually, morally, and religiously, than is true of an equal number of black people in any other portion of the globe."[6]

He taught widely that blacks were ready to go forth in a "missionary spirit" and "to show the people of this country what it is possible for a race to achieve when starting under adverse conditions." They would teach the world the all-important lessons of "reaching down after the less fortunate both at home and abroad."[7] This was the black man's "mission," and Booker T. Washington had no doubt they would fulfill it.

I realized as I read these words that this great leader was not trying to sidestep the evils of slavery. He was giving his people a path out of its devastations. He was giving them a vision that fixed their eyes on God, freed them from bitterness, and drew out the positive impartation to be had from their years of oppression. He did this to elevate the people of his time. He also did it to cleanse the legacy that would be passed on to the next generation. Blacks were not slaves, dressed in rags and mired in ignorance. They were a great and gifted people who had a God-ordained role to play in the world. This was the legacy Booker T. Washington offered to his people.

I recount this tale here because I want to urge the wisdom of Mr. Washington upon you. There are likely hard things your family has experienced in its history. There are likely bruising episodes you have endured. To be a righteous man passing a noble legacy to the next generation, you must help the young to see the redemptive elements in the pain. This is not making excuses. It is not denying reality. It is instead understanding the facts in a way that draws from the heart of suffering the means to ascend.

Men, free yourself from bitterness. In so doing, free the legacy you leave from the cancers that can devour all the good you leave behind. There is a God. There is healing to be had. There is nobility to draw from the worst of times. Let us find these in our stories for the sake of all to come.

THE BATTLE PLAN

1. Does your understanding of manhood already include an obligation to the next generation? If not, why not? Is a sense of calling to launch the next generation something the men in your family line practiced? Ponder how this has shaped you.

2. Pull some men together and think about this principle: "You build a legacy by investing in others." How can you start building this practice into your life? How have the other men built it into theirs? Develop strategies together to get better at it.

3. Think through the lives of the young you hope to influence and fashion at least a brief Legacy Plan. What do you hope to leave them materially? What can you impart to their lives? What are each of their needs, and how can you help meet them? In short, what can you do so that at your death these young people have all they need to live meaningful, righteous lives?

4. Begin incorporating the art of narrating the world into your life. Get help from other men if you find it difficult. Don't be afraid to practice it with your band of brothers. Be brief and clear, but frame the world with loving comments about what manhood is and how it works in life. Don't quit until this becomes natural for you.

5. Think through rituals that you can strategically plant in your life with the young. How can you elevate holidays to make them more impacting? At what other times—entering adolescence, graduations, birthdays, and so on—can you embed simple rituals that impart and remind? Does your ethnic culture and its celebrations help you with this? Ask other men both to teach you their tactics in this area and to hold you accountable for developing your own.

6. Ponder the bitterness that might endanger your family line. What wrongs have been done that are often rehearsed? What wounds threaten to fester? How can you, without denying the truth of what happened, help the next generation to understand the bad things that have befallen their family or race without bitterness, in light of a God who can restore and relaunch? Get help with this. Be diligent about it. You will see victory over time if you give yourself to it.

7. With your band of brothers, contemplate your death. Don't be morbid about this, but do envision the end of your life and what you'll wish to leave behind for others. Start making that vision a reality. Start living in terms of what you want your death to mean. Ask your band of brothers to advise you in this, as you advise them. Build a legacy beyond what you received, a legacy that will help launch the next generation into what they are made to be.

7

The Fire of God

Our humanity is trapped by moral adolescents. We have too many men of science, too few men of God.

GENERAL OMAR BRADLEY[1]

I want to tell you a story. I'm hesitant to do it, though, because it is a story that shows what an idiot I can be. I suppose I should just man up and get to it.

It happened many years ago, when I was on a date in my father's car. My girlfriend and I had been out at the lake and were heading back into town. We needed gas, so I stopped by a station and filled up. If I was true to form, I was talking and posing the entire time, certainly paying very little attention to what I was doing.

We drove off. I'm sure I had visions of TV commercials dancing in my head. My father's sporty car. A babe next to me. The wind in my hair. Me looking dashing in sunglasses and shorts. Cue the Bruce Springsteen soundtrack.

I was in this exalted state of mind when the car, which had been running just fine, began to cough. I knew something was seriously wrong. I turned the car toward home. I never made it. Blocks short of our house, the car died.

Embarrassed, I told my girlfriend I'd be right back. I returned with my father moments later. He wasn't happy. I had interrupted the game and had probably done something to his car. This wasn't going to be one of our warmer moments.

He tried to start the car. Then he sniffed the engine. Then he went to the rear of the car and sniffed the gas cap.

It was at this point that my father told me things about my birth I didn't know. In fact, he told me things about several phases of my life I had never heard before. Then he told me that I had filled the car with diesel fuel.

I remember well what followed. It was $80 for the tow, $300 for draining the gas tank, and more than $500 for removing the diesel fuel from the fuel lines, the injectors, and so forth. I remember all this so well because I paid every penny of it. You should know that the minimum wage at that time was $2.00 an hour. Now, I later worked some higher-paying construction jobs, so I didn't actually have to earn that $880 with 440 hours of labor, but it was close.

There are lessons to be learned here. No, they don't have to do with all the new information my father gave me about my birth. They might have something to do with paying attention to what you're doing at a gas station. The most important one, though, is that the fuel you use for a sophisticated machine is important. Use the wrong fuel and the machine won't work right.

Gentlemen, it is the same with our souls.

Now, I want to be careful with what I say next. You can tell by the title of this chapter that I'm about to talk about God, and while I do not want to offend, I do want to speak the truth. I've welcomed men of every religion and no religion to these pages, and I am thrilled all of you are here. Still, I must say it clearly. We must connect with God if we are going to become the men we are made to be, if we are going to have the fires of noble manhood burning in our lives.

The reason is simple. God made us. This means he knows how we run best. He also designed us to function in connection with him. To try to be good men without him in our lives is like us trying to be elite athletes on a diet of cupcakes and Kool-Aid. It just isn't going to happen.

What I've just said is true of all human beings. Yet I want you to hear this truth and apply it to yourself as a man. God made you a man. God made the nature of manhood. God created the way you think as a man, the desires you have as a man, your strength as a man, and your purpose as a man. He is intimately involved in all that you are as a man, and he is eager that you emerge as a righteous, fulfilled man.

When I say these words, some of you are thrilled and some are skeptical. I understand. I don't want to sidestep any of this. Yet I have a suspicion. When I mention God, most men think of religion. Thoughts of religion then lead them to thoughts of church. This lands them in remembering that hour or so on Sunday morning that hasn't proven to be that fun. Again, I get it.

The truth is that until very recently and in a relatively small number of churches, men have not fared well in their relationship with church. This is why most churches are filled with women but light on men. This is why men disliking church is so well known that there are books and major studies about it. Except for the growing number of churches that have learned to become men-friendly, church has often been a place where manhood goes to die.

There are dozens of reasons why. Here are a few. The first is that church is a fairly feminine experience. The whole thing emphasizes feelings. There is little to actually do. In many churches there are required hugs and greetings that some men see as the onset of criminal activity. You have to know the internal code—when to stand, when to kneel, when to eat the cracker, when to fork over your hard-earned money. Then there are the songs. They are not the kind of thing you listen to on the radio while driving to work. There is also the fact that you are so busy keeping up with it all that there is no time to actually connect with God, even if you wanted to.

Then there is the state of manhood in the place. I've heard the same jokes you've heard. A man-eating tiger would die of starvation in most churches. And the preachers? Some have concluded that there aren't two genders, there are three: men, women, and preachers. I remember a man I knew years ago who looked a bit like a television minister. He had "preacher hair"—highly coiffed and super-glued in place. People would often approach him and ask him if he was a famous preacher. "No," he would say. "I just haven't been feeling well lately." Then he would laugh uproariously.

Now, I have to tell you frankly that these attitudes—as fun as the jokes can be—are outdated. Some of the manliest men I know are pastors and ministers. The culture of cutting-edge churches is changing, and we are glad for it. Still, a feeling that church is a feminine place filled with half-men is one many men carry around with them. I care about it here only because I don't want attitudes toward church to keep men from God.

Yet, again, I get it. I've even heard men complain about the way Jesus Christ is portrayed in most church art. We've all probably laughed about the depictions of him that look like he's in a bathrobe with a sheep under his arm. Then there are the statues and crucifixes that make him look like a tortured vegan. He's wiry, he's desiccated, he's wimpy, and he's cadaverous. I should emphasize he's *depicted* in all these ways, because, of course, this is not what he looked like. These are religious interpretations designed to make a point. I can also show you paintings of Jesus that make him look like he's just returning from a showing of the *Rocky Horror Picture Show* on a rainy night. He never looked that way in real life either.

What is tragic to me about these attitudes toward "Church Jesus" is that they are so far from the man at the heart of my faith. I'm a Christian. I'm a follower of Jesus. One of the things I have always loved about my religion is that it is centered around a man who was fully man. I don't say this because God is usually referred to with the masculine pronoun or because the Bible tells stories about men more than about women. There are many gallant women described in Scripture, far more than we have usually realized. No, I say this because it is the life of this Jesus—despite how he is often portrayed—that has always called to me as a man.

A Man's Man

Run with me for a moment. Don't back away if you are not a particularly religious person. Even if you don't embrace my faith, I want you to see what it is that reaches me as a man in my faith. I also want to tell men who have been turned off to church that there is still a God waiting to relate to them as men.

The Jesus I follow is God who became a man. The big-boy theological term for this is *incarnation*. It means simply "in flesh." When you say loudly in a restaurant that you are a carnivore, you are using a version of this word—*carnae*, in Latin, or "meat." So my God became the stuff that we work on improving in the weight room and that we admire—hopefully—in the mirror. He became flesh. This speaks to me as a man.

He also lived a life that was a grand adventure. I say this because the usual religiousy presentation of Jesus has him floating six inches above the ground. Yet this guy was a man.

Follow me. His mother became pregnant without her fiancé's involvement. Since he was born in a small town, this was the stuff of gossip. Let's be blunt: he was the bastard of his town. At least that was the buzz. It got worse. I can show you documents from the time that describe his mother as a whore.

He was hunted nearly every day of his life. Given what had been said about him being some great messiah, the political rulers at the time set out to kill him. His parents, then, carried him away to Egypt during his early years. Only after some of these corrupt politicians died did the family return.

They chose to settle in a mountainous region regarded by most outsiders as a place of hillbillies. The men were tough and the women were bold, and everyone was strong and raucous and spoke with distinct accents.

You've probably heard that Jesus was a carpenter. It's partially true. The word that describes this in the original language also means stonemason. So, picture the teenage Jesus, increasingly buff, lugging around stones, handling logs, and using the heavy tools of his trade.

In time, he set off from home to do what he thought he was made to do. Remember, he was hunted by assassins nearly every day of his life. He drew a band of men around him. These were no effete scholars. They were laborers, mostly. Some were rough fishermen. One was a demanding tax collector protected by armed guards. Another may have been a terrorist. I can picture them farting and telling jokes and pushing each other into the water as they walked by the sea. These were men. No one had wings. No one glowed when they spoke. Few even had manners.

The movies about Jesus make us think that everyone thought he was amazing until the Evil Empire finally killed him. Not true. He was preaching to a houseful of people once when his family showed up, announced that they thought he had lost his mind, and said they wanted to take him home (see Mark 3:20–21). Thanks, Mom! Another time he was slow to go to a big meeting in the capital city, and his brothers used this moment to taunt him. "Why don't you get going?" they said. "Anyone who wants to become famous has to show up in the big city." The man writing the story then wrote that they said this because "even his own brothers did not believe in him" (John 7:5).

We are pretty certain his father died when he was young. His cousin died while serving him. In fact, this cousin was decapitated for the entertainment of a drunken crowd of royals. Once Jesus spoke to a gathering in his hometown. The people there became so enraged they forced him to the edge of a cliff and almost threw him off. Corrupt officials met constantly to figure out how to kill him. Finally, they figured out a way. They bribed one of his best friends to turn him in. When it happened, all his other friends ran away.

Let's take the story home. Jesus was then beaten by raging career soldiers. They knew how to pound a man. He had six-inch thorns pressed into his skull. He was whipped by a military professional trained for the work. The man used a whip with multiple leather straps, all with rocks and pieces of pottery and iron knotted into them. The goal of this kind of whipping was not to lacerate. It was to pull off chunks of flesh. You may have heard Jesus was whipped forty times. It isn't true. He was whipped until he was near death. The Evil Empire's way of whipping was even called "the Almost Death."

He had spikes driven through his hands and his overlapped feet as he was nailed to intersecting beams. He was already near death before he was put there. He had to push on his feet with the nail through them to even breathe. This went on for six hours. During that time, he arranged for his best friend to take care of his mother, something a good man would do. He then forgave his torturers and died.

Guys, this was a man! This was not the man we see in most church art. This was a true, masculine man. I'm not trying to be cute when I say that his life shows his character as that of all our movie heroes wrapped into one man.

Let me tell you the conclusion of the matter. In my faith, this same man is now sitting right near God, telling him what it's like to be a man. The fancy words for this are *interceding* or *advocating*, but basically these terms only mean that Jesus is sitting near God explaining what we deal with and what we need—as men!

You can see why this means so much to me. Jesus may not have done anything wrong when he saw a shapely woman, but he can represent to God what it feels like and what a man needs to behave properly. Jesus may not have eaten to excess or gotten raging drunk or pounded a man who insulted him into the ground or stolen something he wanted or lied to make men think better of him or betrayed his friends—but he knew what being tempted to do all of these things felt like. In my faith, right now he's representing these things to God so that you and I can be good and righteous men.

Now, having said all this, you can understand why it angers me when a man distances himself from God because some prior religious experience doesn't measure up. You can understand why it angers me that Jesus is presented in the silly way he usually is. You can also understand why I say that a man can't be a complete man without connecting to God. Is my faith only a faith for men? Not at all. But when you look at it just in terms of men, you can see the power it has to make great men. This is why the churchy bathrobe-wearing sheep-carrying version of Jesus just ticks me off.

Gentlemen, we need a connection to God if we are going to be the men we are called to be. We need his fire in our lives. Let me tell you why.

The Alignment

First, everything that is wrong in us as men is a perversion of a good thing. Rape and sexual molestation are the perversion of the gift of sex, which is a good thing. Eating and drinking to excess are the perversion of our hunger drive, again, a good thing. Our violence and rage are a perversion of the gift of our strength and warrior skill, both good things. I could go on for pages. What is wrong in me is what is right in me, deformed. What is wrong in me is gifts from God distorted into forces for destruction, abuse, and damaging lives.

I need God to realign me. I need God to restore my gifts to their original purpose. A man with an out-of-control porn addiction or sexual insanity needs to be put right and restored to a glorious sex life with one woman. He needs his emotions to be tamed and to be put to righteous use. Then he can experience life fully, get in sync with others, and express beautiful things to those he loves. He needs for the perversions and the distortions to stop. God can do this. Godly men can help. I can be set free from what drives me to stupidity, but it takes the work of God to get it done.

Overcoming Wounds

Second, I love the scene in the movie *Black Hawk Down* when an officer gives an order to a man and he responds, "But I've been shot!" The officer glares back at him and says, "We've all been shot!"

My friends and I have turned this into a line of encouragement to each other. One of us will tell the others, let's say, that he lost his temper the other day. He's ashamed and trying to figure out why. After a few moments, another one of us will say, "Well, we've all been shot." The whole group gives a knowing chuckle at that point. Thank you, *Black Hawk Down*!

I'm sure you know as I do that, as our Southern friends say, "This is the dang truth!" We've all been shot. We've all been wounded. One man may have had a magnificent father but may have been sexually abused when he was ten by another man. You may never have been abused but had no father in the home. Our buddy may have had a father and no abuse but suffered from being chubby and nonathletic all his life. Or he's suffered for being blind in one eye. Or never doing well in school. Or being a klutz. Or never having any friends. Or battling attention deficit disorder. Or coming from an embarrassing family or a drunken father or a violent mother or—you fill in the blank from your own life.

These wounds don't have to bleed and deform us all our days on earth. We can get better. We can see our lives restored. It takes the power and love of God, though—and this, again, is why I don't want anything to keep you from the connection to God you were made for.

One of my favorite sayings from the ancient world is this: "Who can bear a crushed spirit?" (Prov. 18:14 NLT). It's a perfect image for the wounds we sustain. It works for us because we are so used to using cans in our modern world. We all know what a crushed can looks like. When we sustain a wound, it is like the partial crushing of a can. The can then has less capacity. It is weaker. It is less useful. It is less suited to its purpose.

So it is with the wounds we sustain as men. Each wound hurts, of course, but it is the ongoing damage that is the real problem. We are "dented," to stay consistent with the image of a can. We hold less. We are deformed. We are also weaker. Wound a man and he doesn't return to the fight as quickly or as fiercely as he did before. Wound a man and he won't be able to hold as much meaning and truth and passion and fire inside of him as he did before. Many men walk this life with a crushed spirit. We need God in our lives to heal us and to orchestrate the healing work of men in our lives.

Let me use a different image for the wounds we sustain. A friend of mine speaks often of the "message of the arrows." He says that we have all seen what it is like when a man gets shot by an arrow. We're all familiar with western movies in which cowboys and natives fight, and we've all likely watched a movie or two about Robin Hood. If we have, then we may also have seen a message sent via an arrow. A message is written on a small piece of paper and then that paper is wrapped around the arrow. The arrow is then fired into something near the person the message is intended for.

My friend says it is the same with our wounds. It is not just that we are wounded—that the arrow hits us—but it is the message attached to the arrow that does the lasting damage. It is bad enough that a young boy is raped. It is quite another thing for the message he absorbs to be, *You are a sissy. You didn't fight back. You must have wanted it. You'll never be a real man.* It is bad enough that a man's father commits suicide. That is a horrible wound. Worse is that the man then lives all his days believing the message, *You are such a disappointment, such a failure as a man, that your father killed himself rather than live with you.* Of course it isn't true, but the lies we believe have great power to deform us.

It's the messages on the arrows that puncture us in this life that do the most damage. How does the script ever get rewritten? We can pull the arrows out of our souls, but the messages stick. How can they ever be erased? How are we ever men again with these messages cycling in our souls? We need a power greater than ourselves. We need someone who loves us, knows what has happened, and has the ability to heal and to arrange for healing events to occur.

The ancient King David said it with great relief: "[God] restores my soul" (Ps. 23:3 NKJV). This doesn't mean to just refresh or encourage a bit. Restoration means that the damage to our souls that might be permanent is removed and a greater wholeness than we have ever known replaces it. This is what it means to have our souls restored. This is also why we need that connection to God that restores and rebuilds and relaunches us to our purposes.

More Than on Our Own

A third reason we need a vital connection to God is that we need resources we don't have on our own. Hear me. It isn't easy to be a man in this generation. I recognize it may be even harder to be a woman, but let me keep my focus on something I know a bit about—men. I'll tell you what is true in my life: I don't have the wisdom to be a good man. I don't have the energy. I don't have the knowledge I need. I don't have the insight or the prescience or the skill or even the amount of love to cover everyone I want to love well. Alone, I'm in trouble. I'm better with my band of brothers but even they can't give me all I need. Nor do I have everything they need. We must turn to God together. We must ask him for his gifts, the gifts uniquely designed so a man can do well what he is called to do.

Listen, I am absolutely crazy about my wife, Beverly. I love her with my whole heart. She is my delight. Still, apart from God I don't have all I need to be her husband. I want to know what she needs. I want to know when she is being attacked. I want to know what might help her, even down to exercise, diet, and wisdom about friends. I also want to protect her, provide for her, and light up her heart with my love.

Do I want this because she is somehow weak and incapable? No. Bev is one of the smartest, most gifted women I know. I want to do all these things because I want to be the manly gift to her I am meant to be. Yet I need help, and God gives it.

I believe in "promptings," little urgings that I know are from God but which are for my wife's good. I've had promptings about a certain exercise she ought to do. I've occasionally had a kind of warning alert about a friend or a situation she is about to be in. I've sensed things to pray about or ask her about or just do for her without saying a thing. She has these same promptings for me. This is what happens when people ask God to empower them to be good men and women.

Beyond having insight for her, I also just need forces in my soul that wouldn't be there otherwise. I would never be as patient or generous or understanding or encouraging or even mentally available were God not resourcing me within. Believe me, I'm not anywhere near where I want to be in any of these areas, but I'm far beyond where I would be alone. God makes me a man, in part, by giving me the inner forces I need to do what I am meant to do. I would be a complete failure otherwise, as I have often proved.

The Authority of a Man

A fourth reason we need connection to God as men has to do with authority. Now, I know many men and women shy away from talking about male authority because the whole idea has been so abused. Yet when I use this word here I'm talking about an authority for doing good and not for dominating. In this sense, every woman I know would like for every man of good intent to have as much authority as possible.

Much of what a man is meant to be about requires a level of authority. Again, I don't mean authority over wives and children and friends. I mean authority to serve them.

A man's primary role is to tend the field of all that has been entrusted to him. He is meant to make sure that everything he's been given thrives and is protected and is helped to rise to its God-intended best. This takes authority, and the kind of authority I'm talking about comes from God.

I need authority to stand guard over all I've been given. I not only mean authority to pray and battle spiritually but also authority to stand at the perimeter of my world and drive off evil. I know we make jokes about it, but I want my daughter's dates to treat her with respect, if for no other reason than because they have met me and sense the power of what is between my daughter and me. I want to have authority to speak gently into my son's heart, not to dominate but to help him. I want authority from God to speak for my family's affairs in business and to back off those of ill intent and to coach everyone entrusted to me for their good.

Let me give you an example I often recount when I'm illustrating this matter of men and authority. When my daughter was in high school, her mother and I had to pick her up at the end of the school day. We did this by entering a large atrium and finding our child in the melee. My daughter and I enjoyed these times together. Often we roared back home down the highway, our favorite music blaring.

As we drove home one day, she described something to me that had happened several times when I entered that atrium. She said that on more than one occasion she had been talking to a boy who had his back turned to the door through which the parents entered. Then I would walk in. She said that often the boy she was talking to would "gentle up." He would get quieter, more respectful. Now, nothing inappropriate had been happening. My daughter wouldn't have allowed that. Yet these boys would change when I walked in— even though they couldn't see me. One of them took a step back. Another actually misspoke and called her "ma'am" though they were both the same age. It had happened repeatedly.

I laughed with her about this, but then I asked her what she thought had happened. She looked at me with a big smile and said, "Mufasa was in the house!" She was referring, of course, to the regal father lion in *The Lion King*. Though my daughter was only an early teenager, she understood that me just entering a room changed the environment for her. I'm her father. I am, until she marries, the lead man in her life. Of course I have authority for her life. Yet I don't want this to be just a natural authority based on size and strength and perhaps financial control. I want it to be authority that comes from God for her life. This is what she knew entered the room with me at her high school. This is what she knew was given to me for her good.

So I have no hesitation talking about men and authority. May every man who is righteous, honorable, and well intentioned have authority for building people up but not tearing them down. May every man of this kind be terrifying to evil, protective of good, and have power to coach and encourage. This, again, is why we men need a dynamic connection to God. He gives us the authority to fulfill our noble purpose.

Filling the Hole in Our Souls

Finally, we need a vital connection to God because he fills the hole in our souls. A wise man in the ancient world once said, "Lord, you have made us for yourself, and our hearts are restless until they find their rest in you."[2] This is true, and much that goes wrong with men is related to it.

We are spiritual beings, and we have a need for this connection to God I keep talking about. If we don't turn to God to fill us as we are meant to be, we live with an inner vacuum in our lives that quickly becomes the source of all our problems. It is our many attempts to fill this vacuum ourselves that lead to what destroys our lives.

Apart from God, we have this aching hunger in our souls that we men in particular will try to fill with every kind of natural thing. We'll try finding the answer for this inner ache by owning things or by being the best at some sport or with money or at the bottom of a bottle of whiskey or in the exercise of some form of power or with a crazed approach to sex. In other words, we start shoving earthly things into a spiritual hole in hopes that the ache will go away. It doesn't.

I sit with a lot of men who have a few years on them and are just starting to become what they were meant to be as men. I'm thrilled for where they are heading, but it is where they've been that haunts me. I see the regret in their faces. Many of them describe decades of trying to fix a hunger in their hearts with everything they could cram into their lives, legal and not. I listen to them tell me about the good times and the fun, but I grieve that it was all done so manically— and sometimes criminally—that it nearly ruined them. They speak of lost wives and remote children and broken health and blown-up careers and hearts that were never whole. Then they opened up to God. Then they started coming home as men. I see the fulfillment dawning on their faces. I just wish I didn't have to see it through the tracks of the pain over so many years.

So, yes, God realigns our inner mechanisms as men, he heals us of our wounds, he gives us resources we would not have on our own, and he grants us the authority to do what we are made to do. Yet above all of this, he fills our lives so we are no longer fighting an inner vacuum, no longer moving through this world like crazed addicts trying to get a new fix to cover the ache. He fills us with himself. This is how he also makes us men.

Wisdom from a Rabbi

Perhaps you can tell why I'm so insistent that men get connected to God. This connection really is at the heart of who we are. So I am fierce about this and have a hard time not raging against anything that gets between a man and the Maker of men.

I am also fierce about another aspect of this. Since men see religion as a feminine thing, and since God and godly men in history are often portrayed in unmanly ways, we often lose the masculine content to faith. It's there, but we miss it or it is papered over by less engaging images.

The truth is that there are great and glorious manly themes at the heart of most faiths, and it is time for us to restore them to answer the masculine crisis of our times. Let me give you one example that comes from the heart of two faiths.

One of the men I most admire is Rabbi Daniel Lapin. You may have heard of him. He is often called "America's Rabbi" because he articulates his faith and connects to other faiths so skillfully that the news media frequently look to him to make sense of the world. Though he is an Orthodox Jew and I am a fairly garden-variety Christian, we love each other dearly.

We also sometimes speak at the same events, and this occurred in Nashville not too long ago. I will never forget it. The rabbi was speaking to a group of Christian leaders. It was a racially diverse group: blacks, Asians, Hispanics, and whites. After Rabbi Lapin spoke, there were questions.

Some of the black pastors began to ask the rabbi about the problems of their communities. Why, they wondered, were there such broken families in the African American community when there were also so many churches and such vibrant Christianity?

Respectfully, the rabbi said, "Because you have had Passover without the restoration of the father." At these words, some of the black pastors began to weep.

The rabbi's answer is typical of content from the heart of two faiths that has tremendous meaning for men but which has largely been lost to our time. Let me explain.

You probably have at least some idea what Passover is. You've likely seen the famous Charlton Heston movie *The Ten Commandments* and perhaps you've learned about Passover in religion classes or as part of learning about your faith. Around 1800 BC, the people of Israel were enslaved in Egypt. They were there for four hundred years. Then a man named Moses arose who confronted the Egyptian pharaoh and negotiated for the release of his people. Because the pharaoh was resistant to letting Israel go, ten dramatic plagues were visited upon Egypt. The final one was a killing of all the firstborn in the land. Yet Israel was told by God to celebrate a Passover meal, which involved smearing the blood of a lamb on the doorpost of every house. Every house so marked would be "passed over" by the curse of the death of the firstborn.

Now, there was more to the ritual in this first Passover, and it has to do with the restoration of men. In the ancient Hebrew writings about this time, we are told that this Passover meal was to be convened by the man. He would assemble his household. He would slaughter the lamb. He was to then eat it with his family. He was told to do so with his outer garments tucked into his belt, his sandals on his feet, and his staff in his hand (see Exod. 12:1–11). This anticipated the release from slavery Israel was about to experience but it was also the way a man dressed when he was ready for action.

Now the truth we often miss here, because we've had the manly content drained out of our faith, is that part of the purpose of the Passover was to restore the role of the father. Think of it. For four hundred years, Israel had been in slavery. They were only valued by the Egyptians for their work. Their families were decimated. They were killed at will. Their children were often murdered at birth. You can be sure women were confiscated for sex and servitude. Their health was broken. They were impoverished. What did manhood or fatherhood mean in a world like that?

Then deliverance begins to dawn. Before the final act of deliverance, God ordains a meal. That meal is convened by the lead man, the husband and father. He calls his family together. His family. Where had that thinking been for four hundred years? He leads the meal and does so as a man of action. He does so as a man prepared to lead his family and people out of slavery into a place prepared for them. He also smears the blood on the doorposts of his house, thus rescuing his family from the curse. Why? Because he's a man. Because God wants noble manhood restored to his long-enslaved people. Because noble manhood is necessary for any people to thrive.

So the black leaders in Rabbi Lapin's talk understood what they, and I, had not understood before. He was saying that the African American church had experienced Passover in a sense—a measure of deliverance through faith—but they had not experienced the restoration of manhood and the father that Passover was intended to mean. He knew this because as an expert in the Jewish Torah he was familiar with what most Christians miss of this power story of faith.

I tell you those black leaders left the rabbi's presence determined to return to their churches and see fatherhood restored. They said the absence of manhood and fatherhood was killing their people, and they would not stand for it anymore. They were on fire. I'm sure lives will change because of that moment.

Let us not miss the all-important point here. Every man in that room knew the Passover story. Yet the implications of that story for manhood and fatherhood had never occurred to them. Why? Because, gentlemen, we have had the manly content of our faiths kept from us.

I imagine that if the implications of faith for manhood had been brought more to the fore through the years, we would not be in the crisis we are in today. Men would have heard what faith had to say to them. The voices of faith would have called men to connect with

God, would have taught how God makes men whole, and would have helped them to build bands of brothers devoted to noble purposes.

◁◆◆◆▷

Here is the challenge for you, then. If you've been distant from God because of offense with religion or some other force, come home. Get connected. It's time. If you are a man of faith but find yourself without help from that faith for being a man, then make the changes you need to make. Good men are standing by to help. Find them. Ultimately, start living the God-empowered, God-healed, God-aligned, God-resourced life you are made for. It is time for your heart to be on fire with the presence of the Maker of men.

THE BATTLE PLAN

1. Start asking God to come into your life and remake you as a man. You don't have to be at an altar to do this. Take a walk. Sit with a friend. Do it while working out. It doesn't matter. The important thing is that you start welcoming a connection to God that leads to your restoration as a man.

2. If you've distanced yourself from "organized religion" out of offense, then find someplace to worship that's a fit and where they speak boldly to men. Your absence is only hurting you, and there are surely good gatherings of godly men in your area for you to join.

3. Pull together some men and talk out your life with God—or without God. Be honest. Hear their journeys too. Ask them to hold you accountable about this whole matter of a connection with God and your completeness as a man.

4. Start reading and watching some people who speak boldly to men in light of God. You'll find some recommended reading

at the back of this book. There are more resources, but get started with one of these and then read other titles that one recommends.

5. Find a good conference for men seeking God and attend, preferably with some friends. This is a huge step if you've been away from organized religion for a while, but it is essential. Don't walk alone. Don't walk without godly men urging you on toward God.

6. Most importantly, develop a history with God. Talk to him. Invite him into your challenges. Tell him your gripes. Jot down "promptings." Turn the material in this chapter into personal prayers. Walk with God as a man.

8

The Ritual

Ritual is necessary for us to know anything.
KEN KESEY[1]

Rituals are important—to men in particular. We need them. We long for them. They allow us to make public declaration of our intentions. They give us a chance to cinch down our determinations and to somehow infuse symbols with meaning that then remind us of who we long to be for years after. This is why some men hang swords on their walls or tattoo Celtic crosses on their skin. It is why warriors wear badges of rank and insignias earned in battles past. Men want to incarnate a vision into material symbols of who they are and what they intend to be.

Rituals are particularly important to boys stepping into young manhood. There is a famous African proverb that says, "If we do not initiate the boys, they will burn the village down just to feel its warmth." Boys reach a point in their lives when they want to belong to the community of men. They want to assume responsibility and have a chance to earn esteem. They want to test themselves as men among men.

This is why I love the Jewish tradition of the bar mitzvah in which a thirteen-year-old boy is made a "son of the covenant." He takes his place among the men of the community and, symbolically at least, transitions from his mother's rule into the world of his father. Ritual seals the moment and reminds him of it all his life.

The journey of manhood ought to be marked by meaningful rituals. Like our Jewish friends, we should mark the transition from youth to early manhood with rites a man remembers all his days. Men should gather. Challenges should be issued. Words that encourage and live forever should be spoken. Prayers and affirmations should be offered. Gifts should be given. Then, of course, vast mountains of food and drink should be consumed. We are men, after all.

It should be the same when a man graduates or gets married or has a child. A new season is dawning for him. He needs the wisdom of the older men in his life. He needs to know he will not walk alone. The lore and skills of manhood should be passed on. Prayers and blessings should be offered, and the man should be celebrated for all he is and all he is determined to be. Gifts should be given, the more symbolic the better. Many animals should give their lives for the glorious feast to follow. Surely nothing less would be manly.

In short, a man ought to be able to look back over his life at any stage and see a succession of meaningful moments when men honored him, imparted to him, warned him, encouraged him, gave to him, prayed for him, and celebrated him. Imagine what this would mean in the lives of most men today, in our age of male loneliness and friendlessness, our age when most men cannot name a single buddy, much less a band of brothers with whom they walk through life.

✺

And so I envision a ritual to seal all that we have explored together in these pages. There should be seven fires. These can be seven candles in a downtown living room. They can be seven firepots encompassing a patio in the suburbs. Or they can be seven campfires in a circle out in a field. The important thing is seven flames, some-how, somewhere.

Each fire, each flame, should be labeled. One is the Fire of Heritage. Another is the Fire of Battle. And so it goes.

Our goal is to commit ourselves to each specific fire being ignited in our souls. I mean nothing occult by this, of course. The fires are just symbols. We aren't worshiping them or expecting them to spiritually enter us. What we are about here is a declaration of intention before God. We are making a covenant. We are committing ourselves before God and man. We want to be men with these fires of God burning in our souls.

Men should prepare themselves for this. A bit of prayer and fasting should come before this moment. A bit of reading and preparation. Just don't fall into it casually. This is a moment to define all moments that follow.

There are a thousand possible variations on what follows, and I urge you to be as creative as your culture and context allow. Women can be invited to attend or not. You can dress up or not. You can write the entire ritual out in advance or not. Men can say words they've prepared themselves or agree to words a better wordsmith has crafted for them. It's a ritual, not a straitjacket, and we want all the creativity and variation that make it meaningful for those involved.

The heart of the matter is that after some honoring of God and prayer, men step up to each flame. They recall what they have learned here and from other books and men, and they turn it into a prayer of commitment.

Lord, I yearn for the Fire of Heritage to burn in my soul. I thank you for my family background. I thank you for my family history, my race, my ethnicity, and my nationality. May it all be a tool in your hand to fashion my life. May any evil coming down through my family line be cut off, and may all the righteous good that you have intended take up residence in my soul. I will walk in the nobility of my heritage. I will learn more as you guide me. I will glorify you as a man ennobled by my valiant heritage. May the Fire of Heritage burn fiercely in my soul.

Something like this should be said near each flame. Other men should be witnesses and should set themselves in agreement. Each affirmation before a flame can be done as a group or individually if time allows. The vital matters are understanding the fire needed, turning to God in prayer, and committing before the community of men to welcome each fire and live it out.

I believe it is also vital that each man receive a physical object that reminds him of the experience. There are dozens of possibilities here. An unburned piece of a log. A framed photo. A ring or another piece of jewelry. Whatever works and is meaningful.

Finally, of course, celebration should break out. Manly partying should ensue.

That's it. Remember that this ritual isn't a conclusion but a beginning; it isn't the fire itself but rather an ignition that should set your life on fire.

∞∞∞

Allow me the privilege of adding my blessing to your life.

May you be the man you are made to be. May our God set your soul afire with his purposes and free you from every bondage that keeps you from your destiny. May the fires of noble manhood burn in your soul, and may you be a righteous light in our generation of men, a great and noble man in your time.

So be it!

Acknowledgments

Often, too, our own light goes out, and is rekindled by some experience we go through with a fellowman. Thus we have each of us cause to think with deep gratitude of those who have lighted the flames within us.

ALBERT SCHWEITZER[1]

In the middle of my life, I encountered a band of men who taught me far more than I had ever known about manhood. This book—indeed all of my books on men—and my life as it is would not have been possible without them.

Decades before I came to know them, they formed a movement that came to be called Every Nation. I love this movement as a whole and am part of it to this day, but it has been the individual men who changed my life with their noble examples and manly ways.

I came to them in crisis. In fact, it isn't even true that I came to them. They came to me when I was in crisis. Then they both defended me and began confronting me about flaws I never knew had kept me from my best. It changed me.

I remember one confrontation in particular. I was furious at some people who had wronged me, and I think I mentioned something about killing them all. This would have been my state of soul at the

171

time. The Every Nation guys tore into me, told me that thinking this way was why I would never fulfill my destiny, and warned me I had better "get right" if I was ever to transcend the crisis I was in.

I sat there with tears running down my face and snot swinging from my nose. The confrontation was over. Typically, one of them then said, "Fine, then. Let's go eat." They all got up to leave. I just sat there. You must understand that all through my prior life, confrontation was the same thing as rejection. To my way of thinking, these guys challenging me was simply their way of pushing me out of the club. Yet as the last man was leaving the room, he turned to me and said, "You coming?" I looked at him pitifully and whimpered, "You want me to go?" He smiled. "Yeah. You're buying! Let's go."

It was such manly moments that rebuilt my life. I will be grateful all my days. So here is to Rice Broocks, Russ Austin, Steve Murrell, Phil Bonasso, Tim Johnson, Jim Laffoon, Coach Rohr, Jim Critcher, Sam Webb, Norman Nakanishi, and, of course, Brett Fuller, my mentor and my friend. Men, we really are better together, and I love the way you burned this truth into my life.

It is a great honor that the revered Scott Hamilton agreed to write the foreword to this book. I have long admired him. Of course I honor him for being an Olympic gold medal winner and figure skating champion. Yet it was the way he carried himself through these victories that first drew my attention. It was also the way he fought through health challenges and fought to serve cancer victims and fought to be a valiant man of faith in the public eye that won me. Fires are ignited in my soul by his example, and so he was the perfect man to launch us into these pages. Thank you, Scott.

Karen Montgomery is my executive assistant and friend, and nothing about my professional life is not better for her teaming with me. She can correct me with a laugh or deal with difficulty without losing her balance and all the while bring fifteen ships into harbor at the same time. She and her husband, David, are dear friends, and I am grateful for all they bring to my life.

Ben Richardson is a social media genius who condescended to work with us. He carries my work much further than it would go otherwise and always does it with grace. He also does it from the edge of the Sahara Desert or hanging from the side of a mountain or while doing something dangerous in some remote part of the world. He challenges me as a man, then, in the same way he challenges me to clarify my message. Thank you, Ben.

Among my rowdy band of brothers are two men who walk with me closely in this business of trying to resurrect noble manhood in our generation. J. T. McCraw and Joe Barker are two of the best men I know, and I am grateful for their skills, their devotion, and their friendship. No one confronts me about Oreos or celebrates my victories like J. T., and I'm grateful to have him as my coach. Fine men, all.

My daughter, Elizabeth, has often been at my side in my writing about men. She edited all of my men's books, gave me valuable feedback, and so esteems what it means to be a righteous, noble man that I am inspired to help make more of them in the world. I tell her she is my favorite daughter. It doesn't faze her. She knows she is my only daughter. She also knows I love her dearly.

It does not embarrass me that Beverly, the queen of my life, has a better understanding of valiant manhood than I do. She thus makes me smarter, wiser, more fiery, and ever more devoted to what I do to build men. When I see her with Leander, her grandchild, I realize anew that we are attempting to restore noble manhood not only for our time but for generations yet to come. I love you dearly, babe. Much of the impact we are having is yours.

Finally, I offer thanks to that merry band who are referred to in my home as "the men." These are all the men out there striving to be good men, striving to do what valiant men ought to do. They have come to this challenge perhaps wounded and perhaps lacking meaningful examples. Yet they have come nonetheless, and they are ascending magnificently. You guys are always in my thoughts. May our God fulfill your every noble, manly hope. I love you.

What to Read

This book assumes a bit of knowledge and should create a hunger for a good bit more. I don't want to leave you, then, without the best brief guide I can give you for learning about the lore of noble manhood from the written page.

On the hefty side—the more scholarly side but the side that underlies all else about noble manhood—are some essential learned reads. The best single compilation of manly literature through the ages is edited by Waller R. Newell and is entitled *What Is a Man?: 3,000 Years of Wisdom on the Art of Manly Virtue*. This essential volume is filled with short chapters by authors as diverse as Plato and John F. Kennedy, Shakespeare and David Foster Wallace. Every man should have this on his shelf.

A classic for the study of manhood in history is *The Feminization of American Culture* by Columbia University scholar Ann Douglas. She makes the unpopular case that the decline of manhood in America has much to do with changes in religion. Fascinating and true, I believe. An equally essential volume is Leo Braudy's *From Chivalry to Terrorism: War and the Changing Nature of Masculinity*. This is fine history, well written and easily digestible.

I also strongly recommend *Manhood at Harvard: William James and Others* by Kim Townsend. This book is the tale of a search for manliness at a time when the frontier was closing in American history and many feared true manhood was endangered. It was a time similar to our own, then, and so it is wise for us to consider the movement that produced men like Theodore Roosevelt.

For books on the restoration of men to noble manhood, I have to begin with *Wild at Heart: Discovering the Secret of a Man's Soul* by John Eldredge, my favorite book on the theme. I also recommend *Healing the Masculine Soul: How God Restores Men to Real Manhood* and *Sons of the Father: Healing the Father Wound in Men Today* by Gordon Dalbey.

I care deeply about the tending of boys. Had I been born at a slightly later time, I might have been so drugged up and labeled up that I may never have functioned normally again. Thank God my father intervened and kept the wrong people from making me weirder than I was. I was just a boy! We have to understand the uniqueness of boys, champion them, and father/coach them into what they are made to be. Mothers have long been doing this nearly alone. Thank God. It's time for the rest of us to join them. I like *The Wonder of Boys: What Parents, Mentors, and Educators Can Do to Shape Boys into Exceptional Men* by Michael Gurian and *Boys Adrift: The Five Factors Driving the Growing Epidemic of Unmotivated Boys and Underachieving Young Men* by Leonard Sax. I also strongly recommend *Raising a Modern-Day Knight* by Robert Lewis and *Future Men* by Douglas Wilson. In this latter book, Wilson calls young boys "thunder puppies." Perfect!

On men belonging to a tribe, I recommend Sebastian Junger's *Tribe: On Homecoming and Belonging*. On men and friendship, I recommend *Buddy System: Understanding Male Friendships* by Geoffrey L. Greif. On teaming with other men, I recommend my own little book, *Building Your Band of Brothers*.

I like books of practical manly lore. Anything by ArtofManliness .com, then, will be helpful, but I find my friend Brett McKay's *The Illustrated Art of Manliness* to be particularly wonderful. I really loved *As a Gentleman Would Say* by John Bridges and Bryan Curtis. I would like to see more of its kind and also of books like *The Guy's Guide to Pocket Knives: Badass Games, Throwing Tips, Fighting Moves, Outdoor Skills and Other Manly Stuff* by Mike Yarbrough. How's that for a subtitle!

Finally, I've mentioned the manly tasks of prayer and spiritual warfare in this book. I don't want to leave you without help. I like anything by E. M. Bounds on prayer. He was a Civil War chaplain who cared for his men and led them well during that bloody time. I also recommend *Shaping History Through Prayer and Fasting* by Derek Prince. This man served under General Bernard Montgomery in North Africa during World War II and later became one of the greatest of Christian teachers.

I had the privilege of knowing Derek Prince and writing his biography. When I would walk into his home in Jerusalem, he would shout, "There he is! He weighs 500 pounds." Now, I will tell you that I was a buff 240 at the time, but that didn't matter to the revered Mr. Prince, graduate of Cambridge University. He was a man's man and I loved him. We fought over cookies, we fought over cognac, we fought over the virtues of American versus British football. God, how I miss him.

Notes

Gentlemen, We Begin . . .

1. Frederick Douglass, and James Daley, *Great Speeches by Frederick Douglass* (Mineola, NY: Dover Publications, 2013), 36.

The Seven Fires

1. *Military Review* 35, no. 6 (Fort Leavenworth, KS: United States Army Command and General Staff College, 1955): 3.

Chapter 1 The Fire of Heritage

1. North Callahan, *Carl Sandburg: His Life and Works* (London: Penn State Press, 2010), 197.

2. If you are interested in learning more about these facts, I recommend the following: Molefi Kete Asante, *100 Greatest African Americans: A Biographical Encyclopedia* (Amherst, NY: Prometheus Books, 2002) and Patricia Carter Sluby, *The Inventive Spirit of African Americans: Patented Ingenuity* (Westport, CT: Praeger, 2004).

3. Randolph S. Churchill, *Winston S. Churchill: Youth, 1874–1900* (Boston: Houghton Mifflin, 1966), 43.

4. Winston Churchill, *My Early Life: A Roving Commission* (New York: Charles Scribner's Sons, 1930), 62.

Chapter 2 The Fire of Battle

1. Natalie Wolchover, "What Would Happen If a Lion Fought a Tiger," *LiveScience*, July 16, 2012, https://www.livescience.com/21619-lion-tiger-fight.html. "According to the Lion Research Center at the University of Minnesota, coalitions of two to three male lions usually fight as a group against territorial rivals, but tigers always go it alone."

Chapter 3 The Fire of Destiny

1. T. D. Jakes, *Destiny: Step into Your Purpose* (New York: Hachette, 2015), 6.

2. Winston Churchill, "Crimea Conference," Speech in the House of Commons, February 27, 1945, https://api.parliament.uk/historic-hansard/commons/1945/feb/27/crimea-conference#column_1294.

3. John Pearson, *The Private Lives of Winston Churchill* (New York: Simon and Schuster, 1991), 20.

4. Pearson, *Private Lives*, 284.

5. Winston S. Churchill, *The Second World War: The Gathering Storm* (Boston: Houghton Mifflin, 1948), 667.

6. Winston Churchill, "Radio Broadcast to America on Receiving the Honorary Doctor of Laws Degree from University of Rochester," June 16, 1941, New York, https://www.rochester.edu/newscenter/commencement-history-winston-churchill-addresses-graduates-by-radio-from-london/.

7. John M. Headley, *Luther's View of Church History* (New Haven: Yale University Press, 1963), 1.

8. Victoria E. Matthews, ed., *Black Diamonds: The Wisdom of Booker T. Washington* (Deerfield Beach, FL: Health Communications Inc., 1990), 3–4.

9. Churchill, "Crimea Conference."

Chapter 4 The Fire of Friendship

1. Tim Shanahan, *Running with the Champ: My Forty-Year Friendship with Muhammad Ali* (New York: Simon and Schuster, 2016), 159.

2. Ulysses S. Grant, *The Personal Memoirs of U. S. Grant* (New York: Charles L. Webster and Co., 1894), 658.

3. Rebecca Hinkle, "The Friendship of General Hancock and Armistead," *The Concordian*, April 11, 2018; Peggy Noonan, "These Generals Were the Closest of Enemies," *Wall Street Journal*, May 24, 2018.

4. Ally Fogg, "Britain's Male Suicide Rate Is a National Tragedy," *The Guardian*, February 20, 2014.

Chapter 5 The Fire of Love

1. John Eldredge, *Wild at Heart* (Nashville: Thomas Nelson, 2001, 2010), 15.

Chapter 6 The Fire of Legacy

1. This quote is often attributed to Pericles. It is drawn from his speech to the families of the Athenian war dead.

2. The tale is best recounted in Charles Coulombe, *Puritan's Empire: A Catholic Perspective on American History*, third ed. (Arcadia, CA: Tumblar House, 2008). Here is the decisive paragraph: "An ancestor of his had been aboard the boat which received the dying BL [Brother Lully], Raymond Lully, when that mystic and missionary was stoned by a North African mob in Tunis in 1316. Lully's last words were to say that there lay another continent beyond the sea, and to admonish his

hearers to send missionaries there to save souls. This account was preserved in the young Columbus' family and made a great impression on him."

3. William Manchester, *A World Lit Only by Fire: The Medieval Mind and the Renaissance—Portrait of an Age* (New York: Little, Brown and Co., 1992), 21.

4. Winston S. Churchill, *Savrola* (London: Longmans, Green & Co, 1899), 118.

5. Booker T. Washington, *Up from Slavery* (New York: Oxford University Press, 1995), 9–10.

6. Washington, *Up from Slavery*, 9.

7. Matthews, *Black Diamonds*, 3–4.

Chapter 7 The Fire of God

1. Omar Bradley, "An Armistice Day Address," Boston, Massachusetts, November 10, 1948, from *The Collected Writings of General Omar Bradley*, vol. 1.

2. St. Augustine, *The Confessions*, book 1.

Chapter 8 The Ritual

1. Scott F. Parker, ed., *Conversations with Ken Kesey* (Jackson: University Press of Mississippi, 2014), 68.

Acknowledgments

1. Albert Schweitzer, *Memoirs of Childhood and Youth* (New York: Macmillan, 1931), 90.

About the Author

Stephen Mansfield is a *New York Times* bestselling author whose works include *The Faith of George W. Bush*, *The Faith of Barack Obama*, *The Search for God and Guinness*, *The Character and Greatness of Winston Churchill*, *Lincoln's Battle with God*, and *Mansfield's Book of Manly Men*. He is a popular speaker who also leads a speaker training firm based in Washington, DC. Mansfield lives in Nashville, Tennessee, and his nation's capital with his wife, Beverly, who is an award-winning songwriter and producer. To learn more, visit StephenMansfield.TV.

Join the **GreatMan Movement**

GREATMAN.TV

GreatManTV

GreatMan.TV

GreatMan.TV

For more about Stephen, visit

STEPHENMANSFIELD.TV

Connect with
BakerBooks
Relevant. Intelligent. Engaging.

Sign up for announcements about new and upcoming titles at

BakerBooks.com/SignUp

@ReadBakerBooks